SHAH MOHAMMED

The Heart Market

How to Build an Emotional Brand

Copyright © 2024 by Shah Mohammed

All rights reserved. No part of this publication may be reproduced, stored or transmitted in any form or by any means, electronic, mechanical, photocopying, recording, scanning, or otherwise without written permission from the publisher. It is illegal to copy this book, post it to a website, or distribute it by any other means without permission.

First edition

This book was professionally typeset on Reedsy.
Find out more at reedsy.com

Contents

Introduction		iv
1	Consumers As Humans	1
2	Gather Emotional Insights During Consumer Research	10
3	Quality and Consistency	29
4	Going Above and Beyond the Core Function	36
5	Sell Experiences, Not Products	44
6	Personalization	56
7	Habit Forming Elements	66
8	Telling Stories	73
9	Speak in the Consumer's Language	90
10	Authentic Messaging	96
11	Building Relationships with Customers	106
12	Building A Community of Shared Interests	119
13	Sell Identity	130
14	Customer Empowerment	139
15	Emotional Appeal in Advertisements	150
Conclusion		163
About the Author		165
Also by Shah Mohammed		167

Introduction

Isaac wasn't just your average consumer; he was a fervent admirer of all things Apple. From the sleek design of their products to the seamless integration of technology into daily life, Apple held a special place in his heart.

Isaac's journey with Apple began years ago when he purchased his first iPhone. Entranced by its intuitive interface and unparalleled user experience, he quickly became enamoured with the brand. Soon, his iPhone was not just a device but an extension of himself, seamlessly woven into the fabric of his daily routine.

As the years passed, Isaac's affinity for Apple only deepened. He eagerly awaited each new product release, eagerly anticipating the latest innovations that would enhance his life in ways he never imagined. From iPhones to iPads, MacBooks to Apple Watches, each new addition to the Apple ecosystem brought him joy and excitement.

However, Isaac's connection with Apple extended beyond the realm of products. It was the ethos of the brand that truly captivated him – the relentless pursuit of excellence, the commitment to simplicity, and the belief that technology should enrich lives, not complicate them.

In times of joy and sorrow, triumphs and tribulations, Apple was there for Isaac. Whether capturing precious moments with loved ones on his iPhone or finding solace in the soothing melodies of his favourite songs on his MacBook, Apple's products were more than just tools; they were companions, confidants, and catalysts for connection.

And so, when the time came for Isaac to make a significant purchase – a decision that would shape his professional and personal life – there was no hesitation. He chose Apple once again, not simply for its superior technology or sleek design, but for the emotional bond he had forged with the brand over the years.

For Isaac, choosing Apple wasn't just a rational decision based on features and specifications; it was a deeply emotional one rooted in trust, loyalty, and a shared vision of a better tomorrow. In Apple, he found not just a brand but a kindred spirit – one that understood him, inspired him, and empowered him to pursue his passions with unwavering confidence.

In the same vein, meet Ashok, a young professional navigating the bustling streets of his city with a cup of coffee in hand. But for Ashok, his daily routine wasn't just about caffeine; it was a ritual—an intimate connection with his favourite coffee shop, Starbucks.

For Ashok, Starbucks wasn't just a place to grab a quick cup of joe; it was a sanctuary—a refuge from the chaos of daily life. Whether seeking solace in the soothing ambiance of the café or finding inspiration amidst the chatter of fellow patrons, Starbucks offered Ashok a sense of belonging—a space where he could unwind, recharge, and connect with himself.

But it wasn't just the physical environment that drew Ashok in—it was the brand itself. From the iconic green logo to the friendly baristas who greeted him by name, Starbucks exuded warmth and familiarity, making Ashok feel like part of a larger community.

With each sip of his favourite brew, Ashok felt a sense of comfort and reassurance—a reminder that amidst the uncertainties of life, there was always a place he could call home. And just like Isaac and his unwavering loyalty to Apple, Ashok's bond with Starbucks was built on trust, loyalty, and a shared vision of a better tomorrow.

In Starbucks, Ashok found a place that understood, inspired, and empowered him to start each day with a renewed sense of purpose.

These stories prompt a fundamental question: How do brands forge such profound emotional bonds?

In this book, we'll delve into the world of emotional branding, exploring the strategies and techniques that turn customers into loyal fans, just like countless Apple devotees around the world. We'll explore how brands can tap into the power of storytelling, user experience, and emotional triggers to build a lasting connection with their audience. By the end of this journey, you'll have the tools and knowledge to craft your own emotional brand story, one that resonates with your customers and leaves a lasting impression.

The Emotional Branding

In today's fiercely competitive marketplace, where products and services seem to blur into a sea of sameness, standing out as a brand requires more than just offering something functional or convenient. It demands forging genuine connections with your audience—connections that resonate on a deeply emotional level. This is where the concept of an emotional brand comes into play.

An emotional brand is more than just a logo or a product; it's a beacon of identity that speaks to the hearts and minds of consumers. It's a brand that understands the power of emotions in shaping perceptions, behaviours, and, ultimately, purchasing decisions. When consumers feel a strong emotional connection to a brand, they're not just buying a product or service; they're investing in an experience, a relationship, or a piece of their own identity.

The benefits of building an emotional brand are manifold. For starters, emotionally connected customers are more loyal and more likely to become advocates for your brand. They're not just repeat customers; they're ambassadors who sing your praises to friends, family, and anyone who will listen. This leads to increased brand loyalty, higher customer lifetime value, and, ultimately, higher profits for your business.

However, the benefits of emotional branding extend beyond the bottom line. Emotionally connected brands are also more resilient in times of crisis. When faced with challenges or setbacks, customers who feel a strong emotional bond with your brand are more forgiving and supportive. They're willing to give you the benefit of the doubt and stick with you through thick and thin.

In short, building an emotional brand is not just a nice-to-have; it's a must-have in today's competitive landscape. It's a powerful way to differentiate your brand, foster lasting relationships with your audience, and ultimately, drive long-term success. So if you're ready to take your brand to the next level, it's time to start thinking beyond features and benefits and start thinking about emotions. Because when it comes to building a brand that truly resonates, emotions are where the magic happens.

Note:

Before delving into the specifics of building an emotional brand, it's essential to understand certain points. Building an emotional brand isn't just about creating compelling marketing campaigns or designing visually appealing logos—it's about fostering genuine connections with your audience that resonate on a deep emotional level.

Building an emotional brand takes time. It's not something that can be achieved overnight or through a single emotional advertisement. Instead, it's a gradual process that unfolds over time as you consistently deliver meaningful experiences and build trust with your audience.

So, if you thought that emotional branding could be achieved solely through emotional advertisements, prepare to be surprised. While emotional advertising plays a role, true emotional branding requires a holistic approach that permeates every aspect of your brand—from product design and customer service to marketing campaigns and brand messaging.

So, are you ready to build an emotional brand that resonates with your audience and stands the test of time? Let's explore the strategies and best practices that will guide you on this transformative path.

***

1

Consumers As Humans

To build an emotional brand, it's crucial to first recognize customers not as mere buyers or consumers but as multifaceted humans with unique emotions and needs. This human-centric approach lays the foundation for authentic connections that resonate deeply with your audience, fostering loyalty and brand advocacy.

When brands view consumers through a human-centric lens, they move beyond viewing them as mere transactional entities. Instead, they acknowledge the complexities of human experience—the joys, struggles, aspirations, and fears that shape individual lives. This understanding forms the foundation for building authentic relationships based on empathy, trust, and mutual respect.

By recognizing consumers as humans first and foremost, brands can tailor their products, services, and marketing efforts to address not just functional needs but emotional ones as well. This approach allows brands to create experiences that resonate with consumers on a personal level, fostering a sense of connection and belonging that transcends the transactional nature of business.

For consumers, being seen and understood as humans by brands instils a sense of value, validation, and recognition. It demonstrates that their emotions, preferences, and experiences are not only acknowledged but also respected and prioritized. This acknowledgement of their humanity enhances the overall brand experience, deepening their emotional connection with the brand and fostering long-term loyalty.

Moreover, viewing consumers as humans opens the door to authentic communication and engagement. It encourages brands to listen actively to their audience, seek feedback, and engage in meaningful dialogue. This two-way interaction builds trust and fosters a sense of partnership, empowering consumers to play an active role in shaping the brand's evolution.

Ultimately, by shifting the focus from transactions to relationships, brands can unlock the full potential of emotional branding and create meaningful experiences that resonate with their audience on a profound level.

Building A Culture

Recognizing consumers as humans shouldn't be a superficial gesture or confined to product design—it must permeate every facet of the organization, becoming ingrained within its culture. This holistic approach ensures that the human-centric ethos is not just a marketing tactic but a fundamental guiding principle that influences every decision and interaction.

At its core, embedding this perspective into the organizational culture means fostering empathy at every level, from frontline staff to top executives. It's about instilling a deep understanding and appreciation for the diverse emotions, needs, and experiences of your audience throughout the entire company.

This begins with leadership setting the tone and exemplifying empathy in their actions and decisions. When leaders prioritize understanding and connecting with customers on a human level, it sets a precedent for the rest of the organization to follow suit.

Moreover, human-centricity should be reflected in hiring practices, with a focus on recruiting individuals who not only possess the requisite skills but also demonstrate empathy and an understanding of human behaviour. By building a team that values empathy and customer-centricity, organizations can ensure that these principles are upheld in every interaction with customers.

Training and development programs play a crucial role in ingraining this mindset into the organization's culture. Employees should receive ongoing training on empathy, active listening, and understanding customer emotions. This equips them with the skills and mindset needed to connect with customers authentically and build meaningful relationships.

Furthermore, organizations should establish feedback mechanisms that allow employees to regularly gather insights into customer emotions and experiences. Whether through surveys, focus groups, or direct customer interactions, soliciting feedback enables employees to continuously learn and adapt their approach to better meet customer needs.

Beyond customer-facing roles, every department—from product development to marketing to customer service—should be aligned around the goal of creating emotionally resonant experiences for customers. This requires collaboration and communication across departments to ensure that everyone is working towards a common understanding of the customer and their needs.

Ultimately, embedding a human-centric approach into the organizational culture requires a concerted effort and ongoing commitment from every member of the organization. By making empathy and understanding a central tenet of the company culture, organizations can build stronger emotional connections with their customers and differentiate themselves in the marketplace.

The Honest Company

Imagine Sangita, a new mom, bleary-eyed and overwhelmed by a sea of baby products. Every bottle and package feels like a decision point in a minefield of anxieties. The Honest Company doesn't see Sangita as just a "customer" making a purchase; they see her as a human being on a deeply personal journey of parenthood.

This human-centric approach sets them apart. By truly understanding the emotional needs of parents like Sangita, they can create products and services that go beyond functionality. They prioritize safe, natural ingredients and avoid harsh chemicals to address the anxieties of health-conscious parents. Their educational resources and support communities empower parents facing challenges, fostering a sense of shared experience and understanding.

It's not about just selling baby wipes and diapers; it's about recognizing the emotional rollercoaster of parenthood. The Honest Company builds trust through transparency and avoids overly commercialized marketing. They focus on being a trusted resource and a supportive community, celebrating parenthood's special moments with personalized milestone trackers.

This human-centric approach allows The Honest Company to connect with parents on a deeper level, fostering loyalty and positioning them as a brand that truly understands the complexities of parenthood. In a world of products, they see the people behind the purchases, building emotional connections that transcend transactions.

Dove

Dove, a personal care brand owned by Unilever, has built a strong emotional connection with its audience by challenging traditional beauty standards and promoting a more inclusive and empowering definition of beauty.

In 2004, Dove launched its groundbreaking "Campaign for Real Beauty," which featured women of diverse ages, shapes, and sizes in their advertising. This was a stark contrast to the heavily airbrushed and idealized images of beauty that had long dominated the industry.

By featuring "real" women in their campaigns, Dove acknowledged that its consumers were not just bodies or faces to be sold products to, but complex human beings with diverse experiences, insecurities, and aspirations. The brand recognized that many women struggled with self-esteem and body image issues, and sought to address these emotional challenges head-on.

Through initiatives like the Dove Self-Esteem Project, which aimed to educate young people about body confidence and media literacy, Dove demonstrated a genuine commitment to empowering and uplifting its consumers on a deeper, emotional level.

The brand's messaging emphasized that true beauty lies in embracing one's unique self rather than conforming to narrow, unrealistic standards. This resonated profoundly with women who had long felt excluded or marginalized by the mainstream beauty industry.

By considering its consumers as human beings with complex emotions and experiences around beauty and self-worth, Dove forged a powerful emotional connection with its audience. Women felt seen, understood, and valued by a brand that acknowledged their struggles and celebrated their individuality.

Airbnb

From its inception, Airbnb has positioned itself not just as a platform for booking accommodations but as a community-driven platform that fosters meaningful connections between hosts and guests. The company recognizes that travel is inherently a deeply personal experience shaped by the unique desires, preferences, and emotions of individuals.

Airbnb's human-centric approach begins with its leadership, as demonstrated by CEO Brian Chesky's emphasis on empathy and understanding. Chesky has spoken extensively about the importance of connecting with customers on a human level and has personally engaged with hosts and guests to better understand their needs and experiences.

Moreover, Airbnb's hiring practices reflect its commitment to empathy and customer-centricity. The company looks for individuals who not only possess the requisite skills but also demonstrate a genuine understanding of human behaviour and a passion for creating meaningful connections. This ensures that Airbnb's team is equipped to deliver exceptional experiences that resonate with users on a personal level.

Training and development programs at Airbnb prioritize empathy, active listening, and understanding customer emotions. Employees are encouraged to engage with hosts and guests to gain insights into their experiences and emotions, enabling them to tailor their interactions and services accordingly.

Furthermore, Airbnb has established robust feedback mechanisms that allow hosts and guests to share their emotions and experiences openly. Whether through reviews, ratings, or direct communication, Airbnb actively solicits feedback to continuously improve its platform and enhance the user experience.

Across departments, from product development to marketing to customer service, Airbnb is aligned around the goal of creating emotionally resonant experiences for its community members. This collaborative approach ensures that everyone in the organization shares a common understanding of the customer and their needs, enabling Airbnb to deliver exceptional value and build strong emotional connections with its users.

Trader Joe's

The grocery chain Trader Joe's has cultivated a devoted following by treating its customers not just as shoppers, but as valued individuals with their own unique needs, preferences, and lifestyles.

From the moment a customer walks into a Trader Joe's store, they are immersed in an environment that feels distinctly different from a typical supermarket. The quirky decor, handwritten chalkboard signs, and friendly crew members create a warm, inviting atmosphere that makes customers feel like they're part of a community, not just another transaction.

Trader Joe's understands that grocery shopping is about more than just picking up groceries – it's an experience. By creating a fun, welcoming environment, the brand acknowledges that its customers are human beings seeking enjoyment and connection, even in the mundane task of buying food.

The company's product selection also reflects a deep understanding of its customers as individuals with diverse dietary needs, tastes, and values. Trader Joe's offers a wide range of organic, vegan, gluten-free, and specialty items, catering to customers with specific lifestyle choices or dietary restrictions. This level of personalization and consideration for individual needs reinforces the brand's view of its customers as complex human beings, not just generic consumers.

Trader Joe's also fosters a sense of loyalty and emotional connection through its private-label products and limited-time offerings. Customers eagerly anticipate and discuss the arrival of seasonal or specialty items, creating a shared experience and sense of belonging among the brand's following. This taps into the human desire for novelty, discovery, and being part of an in-the-know community.

Moreover, Trader Joe's crew members are trained to engage with customers on a personal level, offering recommendations, sharing product knowledge, and even facilitating conversations among shoppers. This human touch reinforces the brand's commitment to seeing its customers as individuals with unique preferences and needs, rather than just faceless buyers.

By creating a sense of community, offering personalized product selections, and fostering human connections within its stores, Trader Joe's has built a loyal customer base that feels emotionally invested in the brand. Customers don't just shop at Trader Joe's – they feel a sense of belonging and identity as part of the Trader Joe's community.

Body Shop

From its inception in 1976, The Body Shop has positioned itself as a company that deeply cares about its customers' well-being, both physically and emotionally. The brand's commitment to using natural ingredients, ethical sourcing, and promoting self-care and self-love reflects an understanding that consumers are more than just buyers of beauty products – they are human beings with a desire for authenticity, ethical values, and a sense of personal empowerment.

One of the key ways The Body Shop demonstrates its consideration for consumers as humans is through its long-standing activism and advocacy work. The brand has been a vocal champion for various social and environmental causes, including animal rights, fair trade, and supporting marginalized communities. By aligning itself with these values-driven initiatives, The Body

Shop acknowledges that its customers are not just purchasers of cosmetics but individuals with strong beliefs and a desire to make a positive impact on the world.

The Body Shop's marketing and branding efforts also reflect a deep understanding of the emotional needs and aspirations of its customers. The brand's campaigns often celebrate diversity, self-acceptance, and challenging traditional beauty standards – themes that resonate with consumers seeking empowerment and validation as unique individuals. This approach fosters a sense of belonging and emotional connection, as customers feel seen and valued for who they are, not just how they look.

Furthermore, The Body Shop's in-store experience is designed to create a welcoming, relaxing, and educational environment. Knowledgeable staff members are trained to engage with customers on a personal level, offering guidance and advice tailored to individual needs and preferences. This human touch reinforces the brand's commitment to treating customers as complex individuals with unique concerns and goals, rather than just faceless consumers.

The Body Shop's success in building an emotional brand can be attributed to its ability to authentically connect with consumers on a human level. By championing causes that matter to its customers, promoting self-care and self-love, and creating an inclusive, values-driven shopping experience, the brand has cultivated a loyal following of individuals who feel emotionally invested in The Body Shop's mission and identity.

In an industry often criticized for promoting unrealistic beauty standards and prioritizing profits over ethics, The Body Shop stands out as a brand that genuinely considers its consumers as multidimensional human beings with a desire for meaningful connections, personal empowerment, and ethical consumption choices.

In conclusion, recognizing consumers as multifaceted humans with unique emotions and needs is the essential first step in building an emotional brand. By embracing a human-centric approach, brands can forge authentic connections, foster loyalty, and drive business growth. This shift from viewing consumers as transactional entities to valued individuals not only enhances the overall brand experience but also empowers consumers to play an active role in shaping the brand's evolution.

* * *

2

Gather Emotional Insights During Consumer Research

Emotional insights refer to the understanding and awareness of the underlying emotions, motivations, and psychological factors that influence consumer behaviour.

Consumer research, also called user research, serves as the bedrock for understanding various aspects of customers, including their needs, desires, pain points, changing attitudes, and emerging trends. This research forms the basis for every facet of a brand's development. Likewise, to construct an emotional brand, the journey must begin with this research. However, this research should extend beyond merely identifying needs. It necessitates delving deeper into the underlying emotions, motivations, and aspirations that shape consumer decisions, known as Emotional Insights. By gaining a comprehensive understanding of the emotional landscape of the audience, organizations can craft experiences that resonate profoundly and cultivate enduring connections.

Emotional insights provide a window into the hearts and minds of consumers, offering invaluable guidance for brands seeking to build meaningful relationships. Unlike purely transactional interactions, emotional connections are built on empathy, understanding, and shared values. By delving into the emotional drivers behind consumer behaviour, organizations can tailor their offerings and messaging to better meet the emotional needs of their audience.

One of the critical benefits of gathering emotional insights is the ability to create products and experiences that evoke positive emotions and enhance the overall customer experience. By understanding what makes consumers feel joy, excitement, or fulfilment, organizations can design products and services that elicit these emotions, leading to increased satisfaction and loyalty.

Moreover, emotional insights can uncover hidden pain points or frustrations. By identifying and addressing these emotional barriers, organizations can improve customer satisfaction and loyalty, ultimately driving business growth.

Another advantage of gathering emotional insights is the ability to create more resonant and authentic marketing campaigns. By understanding the emotions that resonate with their audience, organizations can craft messaging and imagery that evoke these emotions, creating a deeper connection with consumers. Authenticity is key in emotional branding, and emotional insights can help ensure that marketing efforts ring true with customers.

Furthermore, emotional insights can inform customer service and engagement strategies, enabling organizations to better anticipate and respond to the needs of their audience. By understanding the emotional state of customers at various touchpoints, organizations can tailor their interactions to provide more empathetic and supportive experiences, fostering trust and loyalty.

Radiant Glow(A fictional brand): Imagine a skincare brand, RadiantGlow, embarking on a journey to build an emotional connection with its audience. Through extensive research, including surveys, observation, focus groups, and social listening, RadiantGlow uncovers a powerful emotional insight: the desire for confidence and self-assurance among its target demographic of young professionals.

Armed with this insight, RadiantGlow develops a marketing campaign centred around the theme of "Radiate Confidence." The campaign celebrates inner beauty and self-assurance, positioning RadiantGlow products not just as skincare solutions but as catalysts for confidence and empowerment.

In one ad spot, a young professional prepares for a high-stakes presentation, her confidence radiating as she applies RadiantGlow products, transforming her skincare routine into a ritual of self-care and empowerment. The tagline, "Illuminate Your Confidence," reinforces the emotional connection between the brand and its audience, inviting consumers to experience the transformative power of RadiantGlow products for themselves.

Furthermore, RadiantGlow integrates emotional insights into its product development process, creating formulations designed to not only nourish the skin but also boost confidence and self-esteem. Each product is infused with ingredients known for their uplifting and revitalizing properties, such as vitamin C for brightening and botanical extracts for soothing the mind and spirit.

Beyond marketing and product development, RadiantGlow leverages emotional insights to enhance its customer service experience. Recognizing that skincare concerns often stem from deeper emotional insecurities, RadiantGlow offers personalized consultations with skincare experts who provide empathetic guidance and support, helping customers address both their physical and emotional needs.

As a result of its emotional branding efforts, RadiantGlow has become more than just a skincare brand; it has become a trusted ally in its customers' journey towards confidence and self-assurance. By understanding and addressing the emotional needs of its audience, RadiantGlow fosters deep loyalty and advocacy, solidifying its position as a leader in the competitive skincare market.

Furniture Retailer(A fictional brand): A furniture retailer, "ComfortHome," conducts market research to better understand the emotional experiences of its customers. Through in-depth interviews, observational research, and analysis of customer feedback, ComfortHome uncovers a hidden emotion among its target demographic: a sense of overwhelm and frustration when it comes to choosing furniture that reflects their personal style and vision for their home.

GATHER EMOTIONAL INSIGHTS DURING CONSUMER RESEARCH

While customers are aware of their practical need for furniture to furnish their homes, the research reveals that many also experience underlying emotions related to stress and uncertainty during the furniture shopping process. Customers express feelings of overwhelm when faced with countless options, as well as frustration when trying to find pieces that align with their aesthetic preferences and lifestyles.

Recognizing this emotional insight as an opportunity for innovation, ComfortHome decided to introduce a new service called "DesignEase." This service offers personalized design consultations and curated furniture collections tailored to each customer's unique style and needs.

Through DesignEase, customers have access to experienced interior designers who guide them through the furniture selection process, providing expert advice and recommendations to help bring their vision to life. Additionally, ComfortHome offers curated furniture collections that align with different design aesthetics, making it easier for customers to find pieces that resonate with their personal style.

By addressing the hidden emotions of overwhelm and frustration among its customers, ComfortHome not only enhances the overall shopping experience but also distinguishes itself in the competitive furniture market. Customers feel relieved and supported by the brand as it caters to their emotional needs and offers solutions for simplifying the furniture shopping process. Ultimately, the introduction of DesignEase proves to be a successful endeavour, attracting new customers and fostering loyalty among existing ones who seek guidance and ease in furnishing their homes.

LEGO

LEGO recognized that consumers, especially children and families, desired products and experiences that evoked specific positive emotions. Through market research and understanding consumer needs, LEGO identified several key emotional insights:

1. People craved activities that brought genuine joy, happiness, and a sense of fun into their lives, especially activities that can be done together as a family or shared experience.
2. There was a desire for experiences that instilled a sense of pride and accomplishment and boosted confidence, particularly for children.
3. Adults longed for products that tapped into feelings of nostalgia, allowing them to reconnect with cherished memories from their childhood.
4. Children were drawn to experiences that sparked excitement and wonder and unleashed their creativity and imagination.
5. In today's fast-paced world, consumers seek activities that provide a sense of relaxation, mindfulness, and an escape from daily stresses.

Armed with these emotional insights, LEGO kept tweaking its offerings and added enhancements to its brand:

a) Product Design:

- LEGO sets are designed to be fun and engaging and spark joy through the building process and play experience.
- The sense of accomplishment when completing a set, no matter the complexity, instils pride and confidence.
- Nostalgic themes (e.g., classic space, pirates) and collaborations with beloved franchises (e.g., Star Wars, Harry Potter) tap into emotional connections from childhood.

b) Marketing and Advertising:

- Campaigns often feature children and families enjoying quality time together, laughing, and experiencing the excitement of building and playing with LEGO.
- Advertisements highlight the sense of wonder and creativity evoked by LEGO sets, showcasing the imaginative potential.
- LEGO's branding and messaging reinforce the idea of LEGO as a stress-

relieving, mindful activity for adults and children alike.

c) Brand Experiences:

- LEGOLAND theme parks and LEGO Stores create immersive, hands-on experiences that allow visitors to fully engage with the brand and experience the joy of building and creating.
- Interactive exhibits and large-scale LEGO models evoke a sense of excitement and wonder.
- The LEGO Ambassador program and fan events foster a sense of community and pride among LEGO enthusiasts.

d) Product Line Extensions:

- LEGO has expanded into various product lines catering to different age groups and interests, allowing for diverse emotional connections.
- The LEGO Architecture and LEGO Ideas lines appeal to adults seeking relaxation, nostalgia, and a sense of accomplishment.
- LEGO video games and movies extend the brand experience, allowing fans to further immerse themselves in the imaginative LEGO universe.

e) User-Generated Content and Co-Creation:

- LEGO actively encourages and celebrates user-generated content, such as fan creations and MOCs (My Own Creations), fostering a sense of pride and emotional investment in the brand.
- The LEGO Ideas platform allows fans to submit and vote on ideas for new set designs, giving them a sense of ownership and emotional connection to the brand.

By continuously adapting and introducing new initiatives that address diverse emotional needs and desires, LEGO solidified its position as an emotional brand that transcends age groups and fosters lasting emotional connections with its consumers.

Ford Mustang

The Ford Mustang, introduced in 1964, is a prime example of how emotional insights from consumer research were leveraged to create an iconic and emotionally resonant product. At the time, Ford conducted extensive research to understand the desires and aspirations of two key target audiences: young adults and women.

Emotional Insights from Research:

1. Freedom and Independence: The research revealed that young adults in the 1960s yearned for a sense of freedom, independence, and self-expression. They sought products that reflected their aspirations for an adventurous and unrestrained lifestyle.
2. Youthful Exuberance and Confidence: Ford's research uncovered a strong desire among young consumers for products that embodied youthful energy, confidence, and a break from traditional norms. They wanted a car that reflected their vibrant and spirited personalities.
3. Affordability and Accessibility: Despite their aspirational desires, young adults and women in the 1960s had limited financial resources. They sought affordable products that could provide a taste of luxury and excitement within their means.
4. Personal Style and Self-Expression: Women, in particular, expressed a desire for products that allowed them to express their individual style and personality. They wanted a car that could serve as an extension of their identity and sense of fashion.

Leveraging Emotional Insights:
a) Product Design:

- The Mustang's sleek and sporty design, with its long hood and short rear deck, exuded a sense of youthful exuberance and confidence, appealing to young consumers' aspirations.
- The compact size and affordable pricing made the Mustang accessible to young adults and women, allowing them to experience the freedom and independence of car ownership.
- Ford offered a wide range of customization options, including various exterior colours, interior trims, and accessories, catering to the desire for personal style and self-expression.

b) Marketing and Advertising:

- Ford's marketing campaigns for the Mustang featured young, carefree individuals enjoying the open road and embracing a sense of adventure, tapping into the emotional desires for freedom and independence.
- Advertisements showcased the Mustang's stylish design and customization options, positioning it as a vehicle for personal expression and individuality.
- The campaigns highlighted the Mustang's affordability and accessibility, making it appealing to young adults and women who may have had limited budgets.

c) Brand Experiences:

- Ford organized Mustang rallies and events, providing opportunities for owners to connect with like-minded enthusiasts and share their passion for the car, fostering a sense of community and emotional connection.
- Showrooms and dealerships were designed to create an immersive and exciting atmosphere, allowing potential buyers to experience the thrill of owning a Mustang firsthand.

By leveraging emotional insights from consumer research and addressing the aspirations of young adults and women for freedom, independence, self-expression, and affordability, Ford created an emotionally resonant product in the Mustang. The car's design, marketing, and overall brand experience captured the youthful spirit of the time, fostering a deep emotional connection that has endured for generations.

Identifying Untapped Emotional Opportunities

Identifying untapped emotional opportunities is a cornerstone of successful emotional branding. Sometimes, consumers may not associate a particular emotion with a product or service simply because they haven't been exposed to the idea or because the habit hasn't been formed yet. However, through careful research and observation, brands can uncover these hidden emotional needs and leverage them to create innovative solutions that resonate with their audience.

Consider the scenario of after-dinner gatherings, where guests come together to unwind and enjoy each other's company. While dinner itself may be the main event, there's often a desire for something sweet after dinner to complement the conversation and extend the experience. This presents an emotional opportunity for brands—a chance to provide a product that fulfils the desire for a sweet treat and enhances the social bonding experience.

In this example, let's say a chocolate brand identifies this emotional need through consumer research. They realize that there's a gap in the market for a product specifically designed for post-dinner enjoyment—a premium chocolate designed to be shared among friends and family, creating moments of connection and indulgence.

Armed with this insight, the chocolate brand develops a marketing campaign centred around the idea of "After-Dinner Delights." The campaign highlights the emotional benefits of enjoying chocolate together after a meal—bringing people closer, fostering conversation, and creating memorable experiences. Through captivating imagery and storytelling, the brand positions its chocolates as the perfect accompaniment to these intimate gatherings, appealing to consumers' desire for both indulgence and connection.

Additionally, the brand may collaborate with influencers or host events that showcase the joy of sharing chocolate after dinner, further reinforcing the emotional connection between the product and the experience it facilitates.

By tapping into this previously unrecognized emotional need, the chocolate brand not only fills a market gap but also creates a new habit and ritual for consumers. Over time, as people associate the brand's chocolates with these post-dinner moments, a sense of loyalty and attachment develops, solidifying the brand's position in the market and fostering long-term customer relationships.

By understanding and addressing consumers' unmet emotional needs, brands can create products and experiences that resonate deeply, forging stronger connections with their audience and driving growth and success in the process.

Laundry Agent(A fictional brand): In the fiercely competitive market of laundry detergents, a leading brand, let's call it "FreshScents," embarked on a mission to not only meet the functional needs of consumers but also address their emotional desires. Through extensive consumer research, FreshScents uncovered a powerful emotional insight: the fear and social anxiety that consumers feel about the possibility of their clothes carrying lingering odours after washing.

Observing customers in their daily laundry routines, FreshScents noticed a common behaviour: many individuals would hesitate before wearing freshly washed clothes, fearing the potential embarrassment or discomfort of encountering unpleasant smells while in public. This anticipation of awkward social situations revealed a deeper emotional need for reassurance and confidence in the cleanliness of their garments.

Recognizing this emotional opportunity, FreshScents formulated a revolutionary laundry detergent designed not only to clean clothes effectively but also to provide a delightful and long-lasting scent that would instil confidence and satisfaction in consumers. The brand decided to offer separate variants tailored to the preferences of different demographic segments, including one with a delicate floral fragrance for women's clothing and another with a crisp, refreshing scent for men's clothing.

Upon launching the new product line, FreshScents emphasized the emotional benefits of its detergents in its marketing campaigns, highlighting how the pleasant fragrance would leave clothes smelling fresh and inviting. The brand positioned its detergents as a solution to the common fear of encountering unpleasant odours in social situations, promising consumers the peace of mind that comes with knowing their clothes smell clean and inviting.

As consumers began using FreshScents' laundry detergents, they experienced a newfound sense of confidence and reassurance in their laundry routines. The delightful fragrance not only masked any lingering odours but also became associated with a sense of cleanliness and freshness. Over time, the act of washing clothes with FreshScents detergent and enjoying the lingering scent became a comforting ritual for consumers, further deepening their emotional connection to the brand.

As anticipated, FreshScents' innovative approach to addressing consumer fears and social anxieties through scent proved highly successful. Customers not only appreciated the superior cleaning power of the detergents but also formed a strong emotional attachment to the brand, associating it with feelings of reassurance, confidence, and satisfaction.

A Fictional Brand Example: Kagiri - A premium tea company

Historically, tea brands have focused on functional benefits such as flavour variety, health properties, and convenience. However, Kagiri's research team recognized an untapped emotional opportunity.

Emotional Insight Uncovered: Through extensive ethnographic research, Kagiri's team observed that many consumers seemed to crave moments of stillness and respite amidst their fast-paced, stress-filled lives. While sipping tea was often seen as a simple pleasure, the researchers noticed that people seemed to find a sense of calm and grounding when they took the time to fully engage in the experience of preparing and savouring their tea.

However, in today's busy world, these moments of mindfulness and present-moment awareness are often fleeting and overshadowed by the constant demands of daily life. Consumers didn't necessarily express a direct desire for "rituals" or "mindfulness practices," but their behaviours and emotional states revealed an underlying need for experiences that could provide a sense of respite and a chance to slow down.

Leveraging the Emotional Opportunity: Recognizing this unmet emotional need, Kagiri set out to develop a range of products and experiences that could transform the simple act of drinking tea into a meaningful ritual – a sanctuary from the stresses of modern life.

1. **Ritual Tea Collections:** Kagiri curated premium tea blends specifically designed to encourage mindful sipping. The packaging, aromas, and flavours were carefully crafted to engage the senses and promote a sense of presence and relaxation.
2. **Guided Tea Rituals:** Through their mobile app, Kagiri offered guided audio and video experiences that gently walked customers through various tea rituals. These sessions incorporated elements of mindfulness, such as deep breathing exercises and prompts for self-reflection, without explicitly labeling them as "mindfulness practices."
3. **Immersive Tea Lounges:** Kagiri opened a chain of tranquil tea lounges designed as oases of serenity amidst bustling urban environments. These lounges offered a curated selection of Kagiri's ritual teas, accompanied by soothing ambient music, comfortable seating, and natural elements, creating a calming atmosphere that encouraged customers to slow down and savour the present moment.

Marketing and Brand Experience: Kagiri's marketing campaigns subtly highlighted the emotional benefits of their tea rituals, using imagery and messaging that evoked a sense of calm, respite, and present-moment awareness. Their advertisements and brand experiences invited customers to "take a moment for themselves" and "escape the hustle" without explicitly using terminology like "mindfulness" or "rituals."

By recognizing the unmet emotional need for moments of stillness and respite, Kagiri created a unique and emotionally resonant brand experience. Their products and services provided more than just premium tea; they offered a sanctuary from the stresses of modern life, addressing an emotional need that customers may not have been able to articulate directly but one that resonated deeply with their desire for balance and rejuvenation.

A Fictional Brand: Asta - A smart home entertainment company

Home entertainment brands have historically focused on functional benefits such as picture quality, sound systems, and seamless connectivity. However, Asta's research team identified an untapped emotional opportunity surrounding the viewing experience.

Uncovering the Hidden Emotional Need: Through focus groups and in-home observations, Asta discovered that many families craved shared experiences and quality time together but often struggled to find activities that truly engaged and connected everyone, especially across different age groups.

While watching movies or shows was a common family pastime, the experience was often passive and disconnected, with family members absorbed in their individual devices or distracted by multitasking.

Leveraging the Emotional Insight: Recognizing this unmet emotional need for meaningful shared experiences, Asta developed a range of innovative products and services designed to transform the way families engage with home entertainment:

1. **Interactive Viewing Experiences:** Asta introduced a suite of interactive features that allowed families to engage with content together. This included collaborative world-building elements, where families could customize and build virtual environments related to the stories they were watching, as well as interactive quizzes and challenges that encouraged active participation and discussion.

2. **Multi-Generational Gaming:** Asta partnered with game developers to create a line of family-friendly, multi-generational gaming experiences. These games were designed to be played together, fostering teamwork, problem-solving, and shared moments of accomplishment and celebration among family members of all ages.
3. **Immersive Home Theaters:** Asta offered custom-designed home theater installations that went beyond traditional setups. These immersive spaces incorporated interactive elements, such as motion-sensing technology and augmented reality, allowing families to become fully engrossed in the content they were experiencing together.

Marketing and Brand Experience: Asta's marketing campaigns highlighted the emotional benefits of their products, showcasing families bonding, laughing, and creating lasting memories through shared entertainment experiences. Their advertisements emphasized the importance of quality time together and the joy of engaging with content as a family.

In their flagship showrooms and pop-up experiences, Asta allowed visitors to immerse themselves in interactive viewing experiences, multi-generational games, and immersive home theatres, enabling them to experience the emotional impact of their offerings firsthand.

By tapping into the previously unrecognized emotional need for meaningful shared experiences and quality family time, Asta created a unique and emotionally resonant brand proposition. Their products and services not only provided cutting-edge home entertainment technology but also facilitated genuine connections and memorable moments among family members, fostering a sense of loyalty and attachment among customers seeking to strengthen their family bonds.

Leveraging Positive Universal Emotions

Another strategic approach that brands often take to resonate with a broad audience is targeting positive universal emotional insights.

While identifying hidden unmet emotional needs and tapping into untapped emotional opportunities are valuable tactics, targeting positive universal emotions offers a more inclusive and widely appealing strategy.

By evoking feelings of joy, happiness, and love, brands can foster deep emotional bonds and build strong brand affinity. Moreover, these emotions have a ripple effect, influencing consumer perceptions, behaviour, and brand loyalty in the long term.

One of the key reasons why brands opt to target positive universal emotions is their ability to resonate with a wide range of consumers, regardless of age, gender, or cultural background. By focusing on these emotions, brands can create messages and experiences that have broad appeal, maximizing their reach and impact.

Furthermore, positive universal emotions allow brands to align themselves with aspirational values and ideals. By championing themes of optimism, hope, and resilience, brands can craft a compelling narrative that speaks to consumers' deepest desires and aspirations. This narrative goes beyond product features or functional benefits, resonating with individuals on a profound emotional level. By positioning their offerings as catalysts for positive emotions, brands can differentiate themselves in the marketplace, forging a unique brand identity that deeply connects with consumers.

In challenging or uncertain times, positive universal emotions offer a sense of optimism and hope, drawing consumers to brands that provide moments of joy, comfort, and positivity. By tapping into these emotions, brands can offer a welcome respite from negativity and cultivate a loyal customer base that seeks out uplifting experiences.

Coca-Cola

A great example of a brand that has successfully targeted positive universal emotions is Coca-Cola. Coca-Cola's marketing campaigns have consistently focused on themes of happiness, togetherness, and shared moments of joy, resonating with audiences worldwide.

One of Coca-Cola's most iconic campaigns is the "Open Happiness" campaign, which ran from 2009 to 2016. This campaign celebrated the simple pleasures in life and positioned Coca-Cola as a catalyst for happiness and enjoyment. Through vibrant visuals, upbeat music, and relatable scenarios, the campaign conveyed the message that drinking Coca-Cola could bring people together and create moments of genuine happiness.

Another notable example is the "Share a Coke" campaign, introduced in 2014. This campaign personalized the Coca-Cola experience by printing popular names and phrases on the bottles and cans. By encouraging consumers to share a Coke with someone special, the campaign tapped into the universal emotions of connection, friendship, and love. The campaign's success led to its extension and adaptation in various countries, further solidifying Coca-Cola's position as a brand that fosters positive emotional bonds.

Coca-Cola's long-running "Holidays are Coming" campaign, which features the iconic Coca-Cola Christmas trucks, is another example of the brand's ability to evoke positive universal emotions. This campaign has become a beloved tradition, sparking feelings of nostalgia, warmth, and anticipation for the holiday season. By associating itself with the joy and magic of the holidays, Coca-Cola has created a powerful emotional connection with consumers across generations.

Through these campaigns and many others, Coca-Cola has consistently positioned itself as a brand that celebrates happiness, togetherness, and positive emotions. By tapping into these universal emotions, the brand has built a strong emotional bond with consumers worldwide, fostering brand loyalty and creating a unique brand identity that resonates on a profound level.

LEGO

LEGO is renowned for its ability to evoke feelings of creativity, imagination, and nostalgia in people of all ages. Instead of focusing solely on meeting unmet emotional needs, LEGO leverages positive universal emotions to create experiences that inspire and delight its customers.

For example, LEGO sets are designed not only to entertain but also to stimulate creativity and problem-solving skills. By encouraging individuals to build and create their own unique creations, LEGO fosters a sense of accomplishment and pride, tapping into the positive universal emotions of empowerment and achievement.

Moreover, LEGO's marketing campaigns often evoke feelings of nostalgia, reminding adults of the joy and wonder they experienced while playing with LEGO bricks as children. By tapping into this sense of nostalgia, LEGO creates a powerful emotional connection with its audience, reinforcing positive memories and associations with the brand.

Additionally, LEGO's emphasis on play and exploration appeals to the universal desire for fun and enjoyment. Whether it's building intricate structures or participating in LEGO-themed events and activities, LEGO provides opportunities for individuals to experience moments of joy and excitement, fostering positive emotional experiences.

Through its focus on positive universal emotions such as creativity, nostalgia, empowerment, and joy, LEGO builds a strong emotional bond with its audience, driving brand loyalty and advocacy. By creating products and experiences that resonate with people's deepest desires and aspirations, LEGO continues to inspire imagination and creativity in individuals around the world.

Pampers

Pampers, a leading brand in baby care products, has consistently aimed to evoke feelings of love, joy, and a special bond between parents and their children. By tapping into the universal emotions associated with parenthood and the unconditional love for one's child, Pampers has built a strong emotional connection with its target audience.

One of Pampers' most memorable campaigns is the "Love, Sleep & Play" campaign, which celebrated the simple yet profound moments of connection between parents and their babies. Through heartwarming visuals and narratives, the campaign showcased the joy and wonder of a baby's first experiences, such as their first smile, first giggle, or first steps. By capturing these cherished moments, Pampers evoked emotions of pure happiness, unconditional love, and the priceless bond between parent and child.

Another example is Pampers' "Share the Love" campaign, which encouraged parents to share their love and experiences with their babies through social media platforms. By creating a sense of community and fostering a dialogue among parents, Pampers tapped into the universal emotions of togetherness, support, and the shared joys and challenges of parenthood. This campaign not only strengthened the brand's emotional connection with consumers but also fostered a sense of belonging and solidarity among its customer base.

Pampers has also recognized the importance of addressing the emotional needs of parents during significant milestones, such as the transition from diapers to potty training. Through campaigns like "Potty Training Celebrations," Pampers acknowledged the mixed emotions of pride, nostalgia, and anticipation that parents experience during this phase, offering support and reassurance throughout the journey.

By consistently focusing on the universal emotions associated with parenthood, Pampers has established itself as a brand that truly understands and celebrates the unique bond between parents and their children. This emotional resonance has not only fostered brand loyalty but has also positioned Pampers as a trusted companion for families, providing products and support that extend beyond functional benefits.

In conclusion, gathering emotional insights during consumer research is a foundational step in building an emotional brand. By delving beyond surface-level data to uncover the underlying emotions, motivations, and aspirations that drive consumer behaviour, brands can create experiences that resonate deeply with their audience. This process allows brands to understand the emotional landscape of their customers, enabling them to tailor their products, services, and marketing efforts to address not just functional needs, but emotional ones as well. Ultimately, by harnessing emotional insights, brands can forge authentic connections with their audience, fostering loyalty, advocacy, and long-term success.

* * *

3

Quality and Consistency

In brand-consumer relationships, trust serves as the cornerstone upon which emotional connections are built. Establishing trust is not merely a goal but an imperative for brands seeking to forge enduring bonds with their audience. At the heart of this trust lies the brand's ability to consistently deliver on its promises, particularly through the provision of high-quality products or services.

Quality, in this context, refers to the ability of the product or service to perform its intended function exceptionally well, often surpassing the performance of competitors. Take, for instance, Dyson, a brand that garnered a strong emotional bond with customers through its superior vacuum cleaners.

Dyson's vacuum cleaners revolutionized the industry by offering unparalleled performance and cleaning efficiency. They reduced not only the effort required for vacuuming but also provided a level of cleanliness that exceeded that of competitors. Dyson achieved this by designing vacuum cleaners that excelled at their core function—effectively removing dirt and debris from floors—and did so better than alternative products on the market.

Similarly, Take, for instance, a batter brand that specializes in providing ready-to-use batter for making South Indian delicacies like idlis and dosas. In this scenario, the quality of the batter is paramount. Customers expect the batter to possess the right texture, thickness, fermentation level, freshness, and aroma to ensure the perfect end result – soft idlis and crisp dosas. Any compromise in these aspects can lead to dissatisfaction among customers.

Now, let's focus on consistency. If a customer purchases multiple packets of batter over time, they expect uniformity in quality across all packets. If, out of ten packets, one packet exhibits a slightly watery consistency or fails to ferment properly, it can lead to a negative experience for the customer. This inconsistency undermines the trust they have in the brand's ability to deliver a consistently high-quality product.

Therefore, for this batter brand to build and maintain trust with its customers, it is essential to ensure both quality and consistency in its product. By consistently delivering batter of the intended quality – meeting all the criteria for texture, fermentation, freshness, and aroma – and ensuring uniformity across all packets, the brand can instil confidence in its customers and foster solid emotional connections, setting the brand apart from competitors.

When a brand consistently delivers on its promises and performs its core function exceptionally well, it reinforces its credibility and integrity in the eyes of the customer, ultimately fostering deep emotional connections and loyalty.

In summary, trust is the bedrock upon which lasting brand-consumer relationships are built. By prioritizing quality and consistency in their products and services, brands can reinforce trust, nurture emotional connections, and cultivate enduring loyalty among their customers.

Apple

Apple's commitment to quality and consistency has been a cornerstone of its brand identity since its inception. The company's attention to detail, innovative design, and seamless user experience have set its products apart, fostering a strong emotional bond with its customer base.

Consider the iPhone, one of Apple's flagship products. The quality of the iPhone is evident in its sleek and intuitive design, powerful hardware and software integration, and user-friendly interface. Over successive generations, Apple has consistently delivered improvements and new features that enhance the overall user experience, ensuring that each iteration of the iPhone meets or exceeds the high expectations of its customers.

Moreover, Apple's attention to consistency is remarkable. Regardless of whether a customer purchases an iPhone, iPad, or MacBook, they can expect a consistent level of quality and seamless integration across Apple's ecosystem of products and services. This consistency extends beyond hardware to software, with regular updates that not only introduce new features but also prioritize security, performance, and stability.

Apple's retail stores and customer service further reinforce this commitment to quality and consistency. The company's branded stores offer a carefully curated experience, with knowledgeable staff who can guide customers through the purchase process and provide personalized support. Apple's Genius Bar and online support services are renowned for their responsiveness and dedication to resolving customer issues efficiently.

By consistently delivering high-quality products and services across its entire ecosystem, Apple has fostered a deep emotional connection with its customers. This connection transcends mere brand loyalty; it has created a sense of community and a shared appreciation for Apple's design philosophy and user-centric approach. Customers feel a sense of pride and affinity towards the brand, often identifying themselves as "Apple users" or forming strong bonds with the brand's ethos and values.

Apple's ability to maintain this level of quality and consistency over decades has solidified its position as a trusted and admired brand. Customers are willing to pay a premium for Apple's products because they trust that they will receive a superior and consistent experience, reinforcing the emotional connection and loyalty that the brand has cultivated.

Dyson

The company's founder, James Dyson, was frustrated with the inefficiency and loss of suction power experienced with conventional vacuum cleaners due to clogged bags or filters. He set out to design a vacuum cleaner that could maintain powerful suction and capture even the smallest particles without the need for disposable bags.

The result was a range of vacuum cleaners that consistently delivered superior performance in suction power, filtration, and ease of use. Dyson's vacuum cleaners became renowned for their ability to effectively remove dirt, dust, and allergens from carpets and floors, providing users with a noticeably cleaner living environment.

The exceptional performance of Dyson's vacuum cleaners in fulfilling their intended purpose resonated with consumers, leading to widespread acclaim and loyalty. Customers were impressed by the reliability and consistency of Dyson's products, which consistently outperformed traditional vacuum cleaners in independent tests and real-world use.

Over time, Dyson's commitment to innovation and quality in its core product category established the brand as a leader in the home cleaning industry. Customers developed a deep emotional attachment to Dyson's vacuum cleaners, viewing them not just as household appliances but as indispensable tools that improved their quality of life.

Lodge Cast Iron

Lodge Cast Iron is a prime example of a brand that has built a strong emotional connection with customers by focusing on quality and consistency in its products. Founded in 1896, Lodge has been a staple in American households for generations, renowned for its virtually indestructible skillets and Dutch ovens that have been passed down through generations.

From its humble beginnings in a small foundry in Tennessee to becoming a leading manufacturer of cast iron cookware worldwide, Lodge has remained

QUALITY AND CONSISTENCY

committed to producing high-quality products that stand the test of time. Lodge cast iron cookware heats evenly and retains heat exceptionally well, allowing for perfect searing, slow cooking, and baking. This quality directly addresses the needs of serious cooks and casual home chefs alike, ensuring delicious results and fostering a sense of satisfaction.

What sets Lodge apart is its unwavering dedication to maintaining the highest standards of quality and consistency in its manufacturing processes. Each piece of Lodge cast iron cookware is meticulously crafted to exact specifications, ensuring uniformity in thickness, durability, and cooking performance. Lodge cast iron is legendary for its durability. Proper care allows these pans to last a lifetime, becoming treasured family possessions.

Lodge's cast iron skillets are often passed down through families, creating a sense of nostalgia and tradition. This connection to the past builds an emotional bond with the brand, as Lodge products become more than cookware – they become a symbol of family memories and shared experiences.

Customers trust Lodge not only for the exceptional quality of its products but also for the brand's rich heritage and commitment to American craftsmanship. Lodge's transparency about its manufacturing processes and dedication to sustainability further reinforce its credibility and trustworthiness among consumers. Customers appreciate knowing that their Lodge cast iron cookware is not only built to last a lifetime but also produced in an environmentally responsible manner.

Over the years, Lodge has expanded its product line to include new designs and innovations while staying true to its core principles of quality and consistency. Despite these changes, the brand has maintained its reputation as a trusted provider of cast iron cookware, earning the loyalty and admiration of customers worldwide.

Mercedes-Benz

Mercedes-Benz has long been associated with luxury, performance, and engineering excellence in the automotive industry. The brand's commitment to quality and consistency has been a driving force behind its success and the emotional bonds it has forged with car enthusiasts and loyal customers alike.

One of the hallmarks of Mercedes-Benz is its unwavering focus on craftsmanship and attention to detail. From the meticulous assembly process to the use of premium materials and advanced technologies, every aspect of a Mercedes-Benz vehicle is designed to deliver an exceptional driving experience and uncompromising quality. This commitment to quality is evident in the longevity and reliability of Mercedes-Benz vehicles, which are known for their durability and long-lasting performance.

Consistency is also a key factor in Mercedes-Benz's ability to build emotional connections with its customers. Whether purchasing a compact C-Class or the flagship S-Class, buyers can expect a consistent level of luxury, comfort, and performance that aligns with the brand's reputation. This consistency extends beyond the vehicles themselves, encompassing the brand's dealership experience, customer service, and after-sales support.

Mercedes-Benz dealerships are renowned for their upscale ambiance and knowledgeable staff, ensuring that customers receive a personalized and consistent experience from the moment they enter the showroom. The brand's commitment to customer satisfaction is further exemplified by its comprehensive warranty programs and responsive maintenance services, providing peace of mind and reinforcing the brand's dedication to quality and reliability.

Moreover, Mercedes-Benz has consistently pushed the boundaries of innovation, introducing groundbreaking technologies and safety features that have set industry standards. From pioneering advancements like crumple zones and antilock brakes to the cutting-edge driver assistance systems found in modern Mercedes-Benz vehicles, the brand has consistently delivered on its promise of engineering excellence and innovation.

By consistently delivering high-quality products and services that live up to its brand promise, Mercedes-Benz has cultivated a passionate and loyal customer base. Many Mercedes-Benz owners develop a deep emotional connection with the brand, often passing down their vehicles as cherished family heirlooms or remaining devoted to the brand for generations. This emotional bond is further strengthened by the brand's association with luxury, prestige, and a certain lifestyle aspiration, making Mercedes-Benz more than just a mode of transportation but a symbol of success and sophistication.

In conclusion, trust forms the foundation of enduring brand-consumer relationships. Brands that prioritize quality and consistency in their products and services can reinforce trust, nurture emotional connections, and cultivate lasting loyalty among their customers. By consistently exceeding expectations and upholding their promises, brands like Apple, Dyson, Lodge Cast Iron, and Mercedes-Benz have successfully built strong emotional bonds with their customers, setting themselves apart in the marketplace.

* * *

4

Going Above and Beyond the Core Function

The next step in building an emotional connection involves going beyond the core function of a product or service to enhance the overall customer experience. This strategy requires identifying areas where a brand can add value or address pain points for customers, even if those activities fall outside the traditional scope of the business.

Simply satisfying the basic need or function of a product may not be enough to truly resonate with customers emotionally. Instead, brands must aim to exceed expectations by tackling broader challenges or providing additional benefits that elevate the overall user experience. This may involve removing barriers that prevent customers from fully experiencing the benefits of the product or service.

Let's examine how Apple's iPod exemplifies this concept by going above and beyond its core function and dismantling barriers for customers to fully enjoy their music experience. The core function of the iPod is to provide a seamless music experience on the move, which requires the device to be portable, lightweight, aesthetically pleasing, and capable of storing a large number of songs.

Apple addressed these requirements by designing the iPod with a sleek and minimalist aesthetic, making it visually appealing to users. They also focused on usability, removing unnecessary functions from the device and transferring them to the PC to streamline the user interface. The introduction of the scroll wheel revolutionized the way users navigated through their music libraries, allowing them to access thousands of songs with just a few clicks.

By optimizing the core function of the iPod and simplifying the user experience, Apple ensured that customers could easily enjoy their music on the go. People loved the product and found it easy to use.

However, Steve Jobs's commitment to providing a seamless experience for customers with the iPod made him go beyond the device's core function. Jobs and his team empathized with users by experiencing the challenges firsthand. They recognized the struggle many faced in transferring songs between their PC and the iPod, often taking hours and impacting the overall user experience.

To address this, Apple introduced Firewire technology and a user-friendly music management application. This innovation made transferring songs from a PC to an iPod—and vice versa—seamless, easy, and quick. Unlike other applications of the time that required a learning curve, Apple's solution was intuitive and straightforward, enhancing the user experience significantly.

But Jobs didn't stop there. Through user research, Jobs and his team identified another significant obstacle: the process of obtaining songs. They realized that if customers struggled to acquire new music, their enjoyment of the iPod would be limited, ultimately affecting the overall music experience.

Unlike competitors who focused solely on the device itself, Jobs proactively sought to solve this issue. Traditional methods of purchasing CDs or downloading individual songs online were fraught with challenges, including cumbersome processes and poor-quality downloads. Moreover, customers disliked the idea of purchasing entire albums when they only wanted one or two songs.

From the research, Jobs understood the importance of offering customers an easy and legal way to access new music. Recognizing their aversion to stealing music or committing to digital subscription services, he envisioned a better solution that would benefit everyone involved. Thus, the concept of the iTunes Store was born—an innovative platform where Apple would sell digital versions of songs.

Jobs approached music companies with a proposal to unbundle albums and offer individual songs for sale at 99 cents each. He emphasized that this pricing strategy would encourage impulsive purchases by customers. Fortunately, the music companies agreed, leading to a transformative moment for both the iPod and Apple's future.

The launch of the iTunes Store revolutionized the music industry. Customers could quickly locate and preview songs before purchasing and downloading them, all while enjoying high-quality digital audio. This comprehensive system—the iPod, iTunes Software Application, iTunes Store, and the innovative business model for selling music—delivered a seamless experience for users.

In contrast to competitors like Sony, who failed to innovate beyond the core function of their devices, Apple's willingness to go above and beyond set them apart. While Apple didn't own music albums like Sony, they successfully navigated the landscape and introduced groundbreaking solutions. Their ability to leverage strengths in technology and business acumen enabled them to remove barriers to enjoying music and forge deep emotional connections with customers.

As demonstrated by the loyalty of Apple's customer base, going above and beyond in providing additional benefits or value and removing barriers to enhance the customer experience fosters emotional connections and cultivates brand loyalty. Apple's success with the iPod and iTunes Store exemplifies how such initiatives can lead to significant brand growth and customer devotion.

IKEA

At its core, IKEA's business model revolves around providing stylish yet affordable home furnishings that customers can assemble themselves. However, the company recognized that the process of furnishing a home, especially for first-time homeowners or those relocating, can be overwhelming and daunting.

GOING ABOVE AND BEYOND THE CORE FUNCTION

To address this challenge, IKEA introduced its "Home Planner" tools, both online and in-store. These tools allow customers to design and plan the layout of their rooms virtually, experimenting with different furniture configurations and visualizing how the pieces would fit together. This innovative solution goes beyond simply selling furniture; it provides customers with a comprehensive planning experience, alleviating the stress and uncertainty associated with furnishing a new living space.

Furthermore, IKEA recognized that assembling its flat-packed furniture could be a frustrating experience for some customers. To mitigate this pain point, the company offers affordable furniture assembly services, where customers can pay a fee to have IKEA professionals assemble their purchases. This service removes a significant barrier and enhances the overall customer experience, ensuring that customers can enjoy their new furniture without the hassle of complex assembly.

In addition to these innovative solutions, IKEA has also ventured into the realm of home furnishing inspiration and education. The company's website and in-store displays feature vignettes and room setups that showcase different design styles and decorating ideas. IKEA also offers workshops and classes on topics such as home organization, sustainable living, and interior design, providing customers with valuable knowledge and skills beyond just the products themselves.

By offering these additional services and resources, IKEA has positioned itself as more than just a furniture retailer; it has become a trusted partner in the home furnishing journey. Customers feel supported and empowered throughout the entire process, from planning and designing to assembling and decorating their living spaces.

IKEA's willingness to go beyond its core function of selling furniture has fostered deep emotional connections with its customers. The brand is perceived as a knowledgeable and reliable guide, helping customers navigate the complexities of furnishing and decorating their homes. This emotional bond has contributed to IKEA's success and customer loyalty, as customers appreciate the brand's commitment to enhancing their overall experience.

Airbnb

Airbnb, the online marketplace for short-term home rentals, has expanded its offerings to provide a comprehensive travel experience that goes far beyond just booking accommodations.

At its core, Airbnb's platform allows hosts to list and rent out their properties to travellers seeking an alternative to traditional hotels. However, the company recognized an opportunity to enhance the overall travel experience by providing additional services and resources that cater to the needs and interests of modern travellers.

One of the ways Airbnb has achieved this is through its "Experiences" platform. Launched in 2016, Airbnb Experiences allows travellers to book unique activities and tours hosted by local experts in their destination. These experiences range from cooking classes and guided city tours to outdoor adventures and cultural immersions. By offering these curated experiences, Airbnb has transformed from a mere accommodation provider to a comprehensive travel companion, enabling travellers to connect with local communities and gain authentic insights into their destinations.

Additionally, Airbnb has introduced "Airbnb Plus," a collection of highly-rated, premium homes that have been verified for quality and design. This initiative ensures that travelers can book accommodations that meet stringent standards, providing peace of mind and elevating the overall experience. Airbnb Plus homes often come with additional amenities and services, such as professional cleaning and dedicated check-in assistance, further enhancing the guest experience.

Recognizing the importance of trust and safety in the sharing economy, Airbnb has also implemented robust verification and review systems for both hosts and guests. These measures, along with host protection policies and 24/7 customer support, help create a sense of security and confidence for users, enabling them to fully embrace the Airbnb experience without worries.

Moreover, Airbnb has embraced the concept of community building by creating platforms for hosts and travellers to connect, share stories, and exchange tips. The company organizes events, meetups, and online forums where members of the Airbnb community can interact, fostering a sense of belonging and shared experiences.

Just as Apple revolutionized the music industry with the iTunes Store and IKEA provided home planning solutions, Airbnb has disrupted the travel industry by recognizing and addressing the evolving needs and desires of modern travellers. This commitment to enhancing the overall customer experience has contributed to Airbnb's remarkable growth and has solidified its position as a beloved and innovative brand in the travel industry.

Nespresso

Nespresso didn't just sell coffee machines; it crafted an entire coffee experience that resonated deeply with its customers.

At its core, Nespresso's product is a coffee machine designed to brew high-quality espresso at home. However, Nespresso recognized that brewing excellent coffee was just one part of the overall coffee-drinking experience. To differentiate itself and create a lasting emotional bond with customers, Nespresso went beyond merely selling machines.

Nespresso developed an ecosystem around its coffee machines, encompassing various elements that elevated the overall coffee experience. Central to this ecosystem is the Nespresso Club, a membership program that offers exclusive benefits to Nespresso customers. Members gain access to personalized services, such as coffee recommendations, machine maintenance support, and limited-edition coffee releases. This not only enhances customer satisfaction but also fosters a sense of belonging and loyalty among Nespresso users.

Furthermore, Nespresso invested heavily in developing a diverse range of coffee capsules, each meticulously crafted to deliver a unique flavour profile and aroma. By offering a wide selection of coffee blends sourced from around the world, Nespresso ensures that customers can find their perfect cup of coffee to suit their taste preferences. This attention to detail and commitment to quality resonates with coffee enthusiasts, reinforcing their emotional connection to the brand.

Additionally, Nespresso's sustainability initiatives, such as its recycling program for used coffee capsules, further enhance its appeal to environmentally conscious consumers. By providing a convenient and eco-friendly way to dispose of used capsules, Nespresso demonstrates its commitment to sustainability and ethical practices, which resonates with customers who prioritize environmental stewardship.

Overall, Nespresso's success lies not only in its high-quality coffee machines but also in the entire ecosystem it has built around them.

Patagonia

Patagonia is a brand renowned for its outdoor clothing and gear, but its commitment to environmental sustainability sets it apart and fosters a deep emotional connection with customers.

At its core, Patagonia produces high-quality outdoor apparel designed to withstand rugged outdoor adventures. However, the brand's ethos extends beyond just making durable clothing; it is deeply rooted in environmental activism and conservation.

Patagonia's founder, Yvon Chouinard, built the brand with a strong commitment to environmental responsibility. From the materials used in its products to its supply chain practices, Patagonia prioritizes sustainability at every step of the process. For example, the brand uses recycled materials, organic cotton, and fair labour practices to minimize its environmental footprint and support ethical manufacturing.

Beyond its products, Patagonia actively engages in environmental advocacy and activism. The company has donated millions of dollars to grassroots environmental organizations and has launched campaigns to raise awareness about pressing environmental issues, such as climate change and biodiversity loss. This commitment to environmental stewardship resonates deeply with customers who share Patagonia's values and concerns for the planet.

Moreover, Patagonia encourages customers to repair, reuse, and recycle their clothing through initiatives like the Worn Wear program, which promotes the repair and resale of used Patagonia garments. By encouraging customers to extend the life of their clothing and minimize waste, Patagonia reinforces its commitment to sustainability and fosters a sense of responsibility among its customer base.

Overall, Patagonia's dedication to environmental sustainability goes beyond just selling outdoor gear; it is a fundamental part of the brand's identity and mission. By aligning its business practices with its environmental values and actively engaging customers in its advocacy efforts, Patagonia creates a strong emotional connection with customers who share its commitment to protecting the planet for future generations.

In conclusion, going beyond the core function of a product or service to enhance the overall customer experience is essential for building emotional connections with consumers. Brands like Apple, Nespresso, and Patagonia exemplify this by addressing broader challenges, providing additional benefits, and removing barriers for customers. By prioritizing customer needs and values, these brands foster deep emotional connections that lead to lasting loyalty and brand advocacy.

* * *

5

Sell Experiences, Not Products

The next factor crucial in building an emotional brand is the shift from selling mere products or services to selling an unforgettable experience.

"Selling experiences" refers to the strategic approach of focusing on creating memorable and emotionally resonant interactions with customers at every stage of their journey with a brand.

Take Apple as a prime example. When Apple introduced the iPod, it wasn't merely marketing a portable music player; it was offering a gateway to a transformative music experience. Apple understood that customers didn't just want to listen to music; they wanted to seamlessly integrate music into their lives, discover new artists effortlessly, and enjoy a sense of personal connection with their favourite tunes. By prioritizing the user interface, design aesthetics, and ecosystem surrounding the iPod, Apple positioned the device as a conduit for a rich and immersive musical journey.

Central to selling this experience is understanding the aspirations, desires, and pain points of the target audience. Emotional brands invest in market research, customer feedback, and empathetic understanding to tailor their offerings not just to meet functional needs but to fulfill deeper emotional desires. They strive to create moments of delight, surprise, and connection at every touchpoint of the customer journey, from browsing products online to unboxing the item at home.

Crucially, emotional brands also understand that the experience extends far beyond the initial purchase. They prioritize post-sale engagement, ongoing support, and community-building initiatives to nurture long-term relationships with their customers. Whether it's providing exceptional customer service, hosting exclusive events, or fostering online communities, emotional brands invest in maintaining a continuous dialogue and connection with their audience.

Furthermore, selling an experience involves engaging the senses to create a multisensory journey for the customer. This could include the visual appeal of a beautifully designed product, the tactile sensation of touching premium materials, the aroma of a freshly brewed cup of coffee, the taste of a gourmet meal, or the sound of soothing music. By stimulating multiple senses, emotional brands enhance the overall experience and make it more memorable.

Additionally, selling an experience means tailoring the offering to meet the unique preferences and needs of individual customers. Emotional brands leverage personalization techniques to create bespoke experiences that resonate with each customer on a personal level. Whether it's recommending personalized product recommendations, offering customization options, or providing tailored customer service, personalization enhances the sense of connection and relevance.

Moreover, selling an experience entails delighting customers at every touchpoint of their journey. Brands go above and beyond to create moments of surprise, delight, and enchantment that exceed customer expectations at each touchpoint.

Customer touchpoints refer to any interaction or engagement a customer has with a brand, whether it's browsing products online, visiting a physical store, receiving customer support, or unboxing a purchased item at home.

Imagine you're planning a trip to your favourite destination. From the moment you start researching online to the moment you return home, every interaction and touchpoint along the way contributes to your overall experience.

Let's break it down. You begin by browsing travel websites, reading reviews, and dreaming about your adventure. The ease of navigating these websites, the helpfulness of reviews, and the inspiration you find all contribute to your initial impression of the travel experience.

Once you've booked your trip, you interact with the airline, hotel, and transportation services. From the moment you check in to the airport, board the plane, arrive at your hotel, and explore your destination, each interaction shapes your perception of the overall journey. The friendliness of the staff, the comfort of the accommodations, and the efficiency of the services all play a role in your experience.

During your trip, you might dine at local restaurants, visit tourist attractions, and engage in activities. The quality of the food, the ambience of the restaurants, the enjoyment of the attractions, and the professionalism of the tour guides all influence your enjoyment and satisfaction.

As you return home, your experience doesn't end. You may share photos and stories with friends and family, write reviews online, and reflect on your memories. The ease of sharing your experiences, the response from your social circle, and the memories you cherish all shape your overall impression of the trip.

Now, imagine if, at any point during this journey, there were hiccups or disappointments. Perhaps the airline lost your luggage, the hotel room wasn't as advertised, or the tour guide was unprofessional. These negative experiences can significantly impact your overall perception of the trip, regardless of how many positive moments you may have had.

In business, this concept applies to every interaction a customer has with a brand, from browsing products online to receiving customer support after a purchase.

Each touchpoint represents an opportunity for emotional brands to enhance the customer experience and foster deeper connections. They understand that every interaction contributes to the brand's overall perception and influences the customer's emotional attachment. Therefore, emotional brands meticulously design and curate experiences to resonate with customers at each touchpoint.

Starbucks

One prime example of a brand that effectively sells an experience alongside its product is Starbucks. Although Starbucks is primarily known for its coffee, it has brilliantly crafted its brand around the concept of providing a "third place" – a home away from home – where customers can feel comfortable and relaxed.

When you step into a Starbucks store, you're not just purchasing a cup of coffee; you're entering a welcoming and cosy environment designed to evoke a sense of comfort and belonging. From the warm lighting to the comfortable seating arrangements, every aspect of the store's ambience is meticulously curated to create a space where people feel at ease. Starbucks has succeeded in transforming its stores into destinations where individuals can linger, unwind, and connect with others.

Moreover, Starbucks has carefully crafted its menu and offerings to complement the overall experience. While coffee remains the focal point, Starbucks ensures that its food offerings do not overpower the aroma of coffee within the store, maintaining a consistent and inviting atmosphere. This attention to detail extends to the music played in the background, contributing to the overall ambience and enhancing the sense of comfort and relaxation.

Starbucks has also fostered a sense of community around its brand. Its stores serve as gathering places for people of all ages and backgrounds – from children and mothers seeking a comfortable space after school hours to retired friends looking to socialize in the evenings. The interiors, furniture, and layout of Starbucks stores are designed to accommodate various social dynamics and preferences, ensuring that every visitor feels at home.

Starbucks has also leveraged the power of storytelling and branding to elevate the coffee-drinking experience into something more meaningful. The company has carefully crafted narratives around its coffee sourcing, roasting processes, and barista expertise, positioning its products as premium and artisanal. By educating customers about the origin and craftsmanship behind their coffee, Starbucks has created an emotional connection that goes beyond mere consumption.

Crucially, Starbucks places a strong emphasis on customer service. Baristas are trained to provide friendly and personalized service, making customers feel valued and appreciated. They often develop personal connections with regular visitors, remembering their preferred orders and engaging in meaningful interactions that contribute to the overall sense of community and familiarity.

Moreover, Starbucks has incorporated elements of personalization and customization into its offerings, allowing customers to tailor their beverages to their individual preferences. This level of personalization fosters a sense of ownership and emotional investment in the Starbucks experience, as customers can create a drink that is uniquely their own.

Beyond the in-store experience, Starbucks has also embraced technology and digital platforms to enhance the overall customer journey. The Starbucks mobile app and loyalty program not only streamline the ordering and payment process but also provide personalized recommendations and rewards, creating a seamless and tailored experience for each customer.

By focusing on creating immersive experiences, Starbucks has transcended the role of a mere coffee shop. The brand has become a lifestyle choice, a haven for many, and a source of emotional connection and loyalty.

GoPro

At its core, GoPro manufactures action cameras known for their compact size, durability, and ability to capture high-quality video and photographs in extreme conditions. These cameras are designed to withstand challenging environments, allowing users to capture moments that would be impossible with traditional cameras. Whether it's surfing giant waves, skydiving from great heights, or exploring remote landscapes, GoPro empowers users to document their adventures and share them with the world. However, GoPro has transcended the role of a mere camera company by positioning itself as a lifestyle brand that enables its customers to capture and share their most thrilling and adventurous experiences.

One of the key ways GoPro has achieved this is through its powerful marketing campaigns and content creation efforts. The brand has masterfully leveraged user-generated content, showcasing breathtaking footage captured by GoPro users during their outdoor adventures, extreme sports, and everyday exploits. By curating and amplifying this content across its social media channels and marketing materials, GoPro has fostered a sense of inspiration among its customers, encouraging them to push their limits and capture their most extraordinary moments.

GoPro has also recognized the importance of storytelling and has developed a rich content ecosystem around its brand. The company produces high-quality videos, documentaries, and web series that showcase the incredible adventures and experiences of GoPro users, further fueling the aspirational and experiential nature of the brand.

Beyond its marketing efforts, GoPro has also invested in creating a comprehensive ecosystem of accessories and software solutions that enhance the overall user experience. From specialized mounts and housings that enable users to capture unique perspectives to video editing tools that simplify the process of creating polished content, GoPro has demonstrated a commitment to supporting its customers' creative pursuits and enabling them to capture and share their experiences seamlessly.

Additionally, GoPro has fostered a sense of community and engagement through events and competitions. The brand organizes GoPro challenges, inviting users to submit their best footage and stories, with winners receiving recognition and prizes. These initiatives not only celebrate the creativity and passion of GoPro's customers but also reinforce the brand's position as a facilitator of extraordinary experiences.

The brand's commitment to innovation and continuous improvement also contributes to the overall experience. GoPro regularly releases updates and accessories that expand the capabilities of its cameras, ensuring that users can continue pushing the boundaries of what's possible in action photography and videography.

Furthermore, GoPro's intuitive and user-friendly interface makes it easy for adventurers of all skill levels to capture stunning footage effortlessly. The brand's focus on simplicity and accessibility ensures that the joy of capturing and sharing experiences remains accessible to everyone, regardless of their technical expertise.

GoPro has become synonymous with adventure, creativity, and the pursuit of extraordinary experiences. Customers don't just purchase GoPro cameras; they buy into a lifestyle and a mindset that encourages them to live life to the fullest and document their most memorable moments.

Airbnb

Another example of a brand that sells an experience rather than a product or service is Airbnb. While Airbnb's core offering is facilitating accommodations for travellers, the brand goes beyond merely providing lodging—it offers a platform for unique and memorable travel experiences.

At the heart of Airbnb's value proposition are two distinct types of experiences: human experiences and cultural experiences.

Human experiences are central to Airbnb's ethos. Unlike staying in a hotel where guests may feel isolated, Airbnb offers a more intimate and personal interaction between hosts and guests. This connection adds a layer of warmth and hospitality to the travel experience, making guests feel welcomed and valued. The host becomes more than just a provider of accommodations; they become a friend, guide, and ambassador for their local community. This human touch fosters a sense of belonging and connection, enriching the overall travel experience.

Cultural experiences are another key aspect of Airbnb's offering. Through its platform, Airbnb allows travellers to immerse themselves in the local culture and lifestyle of their destination. By staying in homes, apartments, or unique properties owned by locals, guests have the opportunity to experience a destination from a truly authentic perspective. This goes beyond typical tourist activities, offering guests the chance to explore hidden gems, discover local traditions, and engage with the community in meaningful ways. Airbnb's "Live There" campaign encapsulates this ethos, encouraging travellers to go beyond simply visiting a place and instead live like a local, embracing the culture and lifestyle of the destination.

Airbnb also provides hosts with opportunities for cultural exchange and learning. Hosting guests from diverse backgrounds allows hosts to share their own culture, traditions, and way of life while also learning from their guests' experiences and perspectives. This cultural exchange enriches the lives of both hosts and guests, fostering mutual understanding and appreciation across cultures.

Airbnb is also a prime example of how focusing on various customer touchpoints and delivering exceptional experiences at each stage can elevate a brand and foster emotional connections with users.

1. **Initial Discovery and Booking Experience:** Airbnb has invested heavily in creating a visually appealing and user-friendly platform that simplifies the process of discovering unique accommodations worldwide. The platform's intuitive search functionality, coupled with stunning photography and detailed listings, allows users to easily explore and find properties that align with their preferences and desired experiences. The ranking algorithm considers factors like user preferences and property attributes to match guests with listings that best suit their needs, further enhancing the overall user experience. This seamless and inspiring initial touchpoint sets the stage for an emotional connection by capturing the user's wanderlust and excitement for their upcoming adventure.
2. **Reviews and Ratings**: User reviews play a crucial role in helping guests make informed decisions. By providing honest feedback, previous guests contribute to the overall transparency and trustworthiness of the platform, enhancing the user experience.
3. **Pre-Arrival Communication and Personalization:** Airbnb facilitates direct communication between hosts and guests, enabling personalized interactions and tailored recommendations even before the trip begins. Hosts can provide local insights, share tips, and ensure that guests feel

welcomed and prepared for their stay. This level of personalization and attention to detail helps build anticipation and a sense of connection with the host and the local community.

4. **Check-In and Accommodation Experience:** Airbnb has implemented stringent standards and verification processes for its "Airbnb Plus" and "Airbnb Luxe" listings, ensuring that guests can expect high-quality accommodations and exceptional hospitality. From seamless check-in processes to thoughtfully designed spaces, every aspect of the accommodation experience is curated to create a memorable and unique stay. By delivering on these promises, Airbnb fosters trust and a sense of delight, further strengthening the emotional bond with its users.

5. **Accommodation Quality**: Airbnb maintains high standards for accommodation quality, encouraging hosts to accurately represent their properties and provide clean, comfortable spaces for guests. User reviews and ratings help ensure accountability and transparency, allowing guests to make informed decisions.

6. **Support Services**: In the event of any issues or concerns during their stay, Airbnb offers responsive customer support services to assist guests. This includes 24/7 support via phone, email, or live chat, as well as a robust resolution process for resolving disputes or addressing emergencies.

7. **Payment System**: Airbnb's streamlined payment system eliminates the awkwardness and inconvenience associated with in-person cash exchanges between guests and hosts. This custom-built system ensures secure and hassle-free transactions, enhancing trust and peace of mind for both parties.

8. **Dynamic Pricing Suggestions**: Airbnb goes beyond merely listing properties by offering hosts insights into pricing strategies. The platform suggests optimal pricing based on factors like location, seasonality, and property type, empowering hosts to maximize their earning potential and providing guests with competitive rates.

9. **Local Experiences and Immersion:** One of the key differentiators for Airbnb is its "Experiences" platform, which allows users to book curated activities and tours hosted by local experts. These experiences provide

SELL EXPERIENCES, NOT PRODUCTS

an authentic and immersive way for travellers to connect with the local culture, traditions, and communities. By facilitating these meaningful connections, Airbnb transcends the role of a mere accommodation provider and becomes a catalyst for creating cherished memories and fostering a deeper appreciation for diverse cultures.

10. **Safety Measures**: Airbnb prioritizes the safety and well-being of both guests and hosts. The platform implements robust safety measures, such as identity verification and secure messaging, to mitigate risks and ensure a secure environment for all users.

11. **Post-Stay Feedback**: After their stay, guests are encouraged to provide feedback and reviews on their experience. This not only helps future guests make informed decisions but also allows Airbnb to continuously improve its platform and services based on user feedback.

By prioritizing the user experience at each touchpoint, Airbnb creates a seamless and enjoyable journey for guests, fostering trust, satisfaction, and loyalty. This emphasis on providing exceptional experiences contributes to Airbnb's reputation as a trusted and beloved brand in the travel industry.

What sets Airbnb apart in delivering memorable experiences at each point is rooted in the design thinking approach embraced by both Chesky and Joe Gebbia. They meticulously consider every aspect from the user's perspective. One of Chesky's methods for determining the experience a company should deliver at each touchpoint is to surpass present customer needs.

Chesky envisions a hierarchy of experiences, starting with a 5-star standard and continually raising the bar. For instance, at the 5-star level, a seamless check-in process where the guest faces no issues may suffice. But Chesky's imagination doesn't stop there. He questions what a 6-star or even a 7-star experience would entail.

A 6-star experience might involve the host warmly welcoming the guest with a personalized gift and providing thoughtful amenities like stocked toiletries and refreshments. However, Chesky pushes further, contemplating a 7-star experience where hosts go above and beyond to cater to guests' unique preferences and desires. This could include offering access to the entire kitchen, arranging special activities or equipment, or facilitating bookings for local experiences.

This approach of continually exceeding expectations at every touchpoint exemplifies Airbnb's commitment to delivering unparalleled experiences that leave a lasting impression on guests.

Lexus

When a potential customer first encounters Lexus, whether through advertising, a showroom visit, or an online platform, the brand emphasizes sophistication, elegance, and quality. Through meticulously crafted marketing campaigns and visually stunning advertisements, Lexus sets the stage for a premium experience.

At the showroom, every aspect is carefully designed to immerse the customer in the luxury lifestyle associated with the brand. From the elegant interior decor to the personalized attention of knowledgeable sales representatives, every touchpoint is curated to evoke a sense of exclusivity and refinement.

During the test drive, the customer is not just evaluating the performance of the vehicle but also experiencing the craftsmanship, comfort, and innovative features that define the Lexus driving experience. Sales associates are trained to highlight key features and address any concerns, ensuring that the customer feels confident and excited about their potential purchase.

Once the decision to purchase is made, the buying process is streamlined and hassle-free. Lexus dealerships offer concierge services, expedited paperwork, and flexible financing options, making the experience convenient and stress-free for the customer.

After the purchase, the relationship with Lexus continues through ongoing customer support and service. The brand prioritizes proactive communication, personalized assistance, and prompt resolution of any issues or concerns. Whether it's scheduling routine maintenance or addressing unexpected repairs, Lexus owners feel valued and well taken care of.

Furthermore, Lexus goes beyond the traditional dealership experience by hosting exclusive events, offering luxury perks, and providing access to premium services such as valet parking and complimentary car washes. These additional touchpoints deepen the emotional connection between the customer and the brand, fostering loyalty and advocacy.

Overall, Lexus exemplifies how selling an experience at each customer touchpoint can create a strong emotional bond that transcends the product itself, elevating the brand to a lifestyle choice synonymous with luxury, sophistication, and unparalleled customer satisfaction.

In conclusion, the shift from selling products or services to selling unforgettable experiences is a hallmark of emotional brands. By prioritizing immersive interactions, understanding customer desires, and delighting them at every touchpoint, these brands forge deep emotional connections that foster loyalty and advocacy. The meticulous curation of experiences, from initial research to post-purchase engagement, ensures that every interaction leaves a lasting impression, reinforcing the brand's identity and solidifying its place in the hearts of consumers.

* * *

6

Personalization

Personalization is a powerful factor in building an emotional brand connection with customers. By tailoring experiences and offerings to individual preferences and needs, brands can create a sense of relevance, exclusivity, and emotional resonance that fosters deep loyalty and affinity.

At its core, personalization acknowledges that every customer is unique, with distinct interests, values, and expectations. By recognizing and catering to these individual needs, brands demonstrate a level of understanding and care that transcends a purely transactional relationship. This personalized approach makes customers feel valued, understood, and appreciated, contributing to a deeper emotional bond with the brand.

Benefits of Personalization:

1. **Customized Experiences**: Personalization allows brands to deliver customized experiences to each customer based on their past interactions, demographics, purchase history, and preferences. This can include personalized product recommendations, targeted marketing messages, and tailored content that speaks directly to the individual's interests and needs.
2. **Enhanced Engagement**: By personalizing the brand experience, companies can increase customer engagement and satisfaction. When

customers feel that a brand understands their preferences and values, they are more likely to engage with the brand's content, products, and services. This leads to higher levels of loyalty and advocacy.

3. **Building Emotional Connections**: Personalization enables brands to connect with customers on an emotional level by demonstrating empathy, understanding, and care. When a brand delivers personalized experiences that anticipate and fulfill customers' needs, it fosters feelings of appreciation, trust, and loyalty.
4. **Increased Relevance**: Personalization ensures that marketing messages and communications are relevant and timely, reducing the likelihood of customer fatigue or disengagement. By delivering the right message to the right person at the right time, brands can capture attention, drive conversions, and build stronger relationships with their audience.
5. **Empowerment and Control**: Personalization empowers customers by giving them control over their interactions with the brand. By allowing customers to customize their preferences, manage their accounts, and choose their communication channels, brands demonstrate respect for individual autonomy and preferences.
6. **Enhanced Brand Loyalty:** Personalized experiences foster a stronger emotional connection with the brand, leading to increased customer loyalty and advocacy.
7. **Improved Conversion Rates:** By targeting marketing messages and product recommendations to specific customer segments, brands can increase conversion rates and sales.
8. **Deeper Customer Insights:** Personalization allows brands to gather valuable data on customer behavior and preferences. This data can be used to refine marketing strategies, improve product offerings, and personalize the customer journey further.

Strategies for Personalization:

1. **Data-Driven Personalization**: Gather data from various sources, includ-

ing website interactions, purchase history, demographic information, and customer feedback. Analyze this data to gain insights into customer preferences, behaviour patterns, and interests. Based on data, personalize communication, product recommendations, and website content.

2. **Segmentation**: Divide your audience into distinct segments based on common characteristics such as demographics, psychographics, purchasing behaviour, or lifecycle stage. This segmentation allows you to tailor your messaging and offers to specific groups, increasing relevance and engagement.
3. **Dynamic Content**: Use dynamic content blocks to personalize website pages, emails, and marketing materials based on individual customer attributes or behaviours. This could include personalized product recommendations, tailored messaging, or customized imagery.
4. **Recommendation Engines**: Implement recommendation engines that use algorithms to analyze customer data and suggest relevant products, content, or services. These recommendations can be displayed on your website, in email campaigns, or within your mobile app to drive cross-selling and upselling opportunities.
5. **Behavioural Targeting:** Track customer behaviour across channels and use this information to deliver targeted messages or offers based on individual interactions.
6. **Personalized Communications**: Craft personalized communications that speak directly to the recipient's interests, preferences, or past interactions with your brand. This could include personalized email campaigns, SMS messages, or social media interactions that reflect the individual's unique needs and interests.
7. **Loyalty Programs**: Develop loyalty programs that reward customers for their engagement and encourage repeat purchases. Personalize rewards and incentives based on each customer's purchasing history, preferences, or level of engagement with your brand.
8. **Cross-Channel Consistency**: Ensure consistency across all customer touchpoints, including your website, mobile app, social media channels, and physical stores. Use integrated customer data to deliver a seamless

and cohesive experience across channels, reinforcing your brand identity and personalization efforts.
9. **Interactive Experiences:** Create interactive experiences that allow customers to personalize their journey. This could involve product configurators, quizzes, or preference surveys.
10. **Personalized Customer Service:** Train customer service representatives to personalize their interactions based on customer data and past interactions.
11. **Continuous Optimization**: Continuously monitor and optimize your personalization efforts based on customer feedback, performance metrics, and market trends. Test different personalization strategies, messages, and offers to identify what resonates best with your audience and adjust your approach accordingly.
12. **Privacy and Consent**: Respect customer privacy and preferences by obtaining explicit consent for data collection and personalization efforts. Be transparent about how customer data is used and give customers control over their data through privacy settings and preferences.

By implementing these strategies effectively, brands can create personalized experiences that resonate with customers, drive engagement and loyalty, and ultimately, lead to business growth and success.

Netflix

Netflix revolutionized the streaming industry by harnessing the power of personalization to create a tailored and immersive entertainment experience for its users. At the heart of Netflix's success lies its AI-powered recommendation algorithms, which analyze users' viewing history, preferences, and behaviour to suggest TV shows and movies that align with their tastes and interests.

These recommendation algorithms consider various factors, such as the shows and movies a user has watched, how they interacted with them (e.g., pausing, rewinding, skipping), search history, ratings, and saved content lists. The goal is to help users discover content they'll enjoy and maximize their long-term satisfaction. This approach is particularly challenging due to the uniqueness of each user, their diverse interests, and the need for recommendations when users are unsure of what to watch.

To achieve this, Netflix employs a sophisticated set of machine-learning models that generate personalized recommendations for different sections of the homepage. From choosing the first video prominently displayed at the top of the homepage to ranking already-watched content for potential continuation and suggesting new content, each algorithm contributes to creating a customized viewing experience. Additionally, messages, notifications, and search results are personalized using recommendation techniques.

Netflix also factors in additional variables like user location, time of day, and device type to make recommendations more relevant. The algorithm utilizes collaborative filtering to identify similarities between users and items, constantly refining its recommendations based on these relationships.

Furthermore, Netflix's original content, known as Netflix Originals, is recommended based on user behaviour and viewing habits. The platform's algorithm analyzes user data to suggest the most relevant Netflix Originals likely to capture the user's interest.

The platform also offers personalized user profiles, allowing multiple users on a single account to have a customized experience. Each profile's viewing history and saved content lists inform recommendations, ensuring that each user receives tailored suggestions.

Netflix's personalization extends beyond content recommendations to features like auto-play, which predicts the next episode a user is likely to watch based on their viewing habits, and personalized posters, which are tailored to reflect the elements of shows and movies the user has previously enjoyed. Another feature is personalized trailers for shows and movies, where the algorithm selects scenes that are most likely to grab the attention of individual users. This tailored approach ensures that each user receives a unique trailer, maximizing engagement and interest.

Moreover, Netflix offers localized content to cater to the diverse preferences and cultural backgrounds of its global audience. By analyzing user data and demographics, Netflix can recommend content that resonates with specific regions or language preferences, making the viewing experience more relevant and enjoyable for users around the world.

Interactive elements, such as interactive storytelling formats or choose-your-own-adventure narratives, further personalize the viewing experience by allowing users to actively participate in the storytelling process. By offering interactive features, Netflix empowers users to engage with content in new and exciting ways, fostering a deeper connection with the platform and the content they consume.

Furthermore, Netflix's recommendation algorithms analyze user behavior to suggest relevant behind-the-scenes content and interviews based on individual preferences and interests. This curated approach enables users to explore additional content related to their favourite shows and movies, enhancing their overall viewing experience.

In essence, Netflix's commitment to personalization has transformed the way users engage with content, enhancing their viewing experience, driving member satisfaction, and ultimately increasing retention rates, solidifying its position as a leader in the streaming industry.

Amazon Prime

Amazon Prime has mastered the art of personalization, crafting an emotionally resonant experience that extends far beyond the functional benefits of its membership program. From the moment customers sign up, they embark on a journey of personalized discovery and tailored experiences that foster a deep sense of connection and affinity with the Amazon brand.

The personalization begins with curated product recommendations, meticulously tailored to each customer's browsing history, purchase patterns, and preferences. As customers explore Amazon's vast catalogue, they feel understood and valued, as the platform seemingly anticipates their unique interests and needs, making the shopping experience efficient and enjoyable.

This personalized touch extends seamlessly to Amazon Prime's entertainment offerings, with Prime Video providing a curated selection of movies and shows tailored to each user's viewing habits and moods. Customers feel a sense of emotional resonance, as though the platform truly understands their unique tastes and desires for entertainment.

But Amazon Prime's personalization transcends mere recommendations. Customers can create personalized profiles, avatars, and even customize their homepages, fostering a sense of ownership and identity with the Amazon experience. This level of personalization makes customers feel as though the brand is truly their own, deepening the emotional bond.

As customers navigate the Prime ecosystem, they encounter personalized shipping and delivery options, tailored to their preferences and lifestyles. From preferred delivery windows to personalized packaging, Amazon Prime creates a sense of convenience and exclusivity, catering to each individual's unique needs.

Voice-based personalization further enhances the emotional connection, as Alexa, Amazon's virtual assistant, learns and adapts to each customer's speech patterns, preferences, and habits, creating a seamless and personalized interaction that feels like a true personal assistant.

Amazon Prime's personalization extends to subscriptions and services, with offerings like Subscribe & Save anticipating and catering to individual consumption patterns, fostering a sense of emotional attachment and convenience.

Even in the realm of gifting, Amazon Prime shines with personalized recommendations, gift wrapping, and messaging options, allowing customers to express their affection and consideration for loved ones in a thoughtful and personalized way.

Moreover, Amazon Prime fosters personalized community and social connections, enabling customers to join interest-based groups, follow influencers, and engage with like-minded individuals, creating a sense of belonging and emotional resonance around shared passions and interests.

Through this multifaceted approach to personalization, Amazon Prime has created an emotional brand connection that transcends transactional relationships. Customers feel a sense of personal investment, identity, and emotional resonance with the Amazon brand, fostering loyalty, advocacy, and a deeper emotional bond that extends far beyond the functional benefits of the membership program.

Patagonia

Patagonia isn't just a clothing brand; it's a community built around a shared love for the outdoors. Their understanding of their customers goes beyond demographics and delves into their passions and aspirations. Here's how Patagonia utilizes personalization to build a strong emotional connection with its customers:

Customization Options: Patagonia offers customization services for certain products, allowing customers to personalize items such as jackets, backpacks, and apparel with embroidered logos, patches, or monograms. This customization feature enables customers to create unique and personalized products that reflect their individual style and preferences.

Fit Finder and Body Scan Technology: Patagonia offers a Fit Finder tool on their website and in some retail stores. This tool uses a combination of user-submitted information and body scan technology (available in select stores) to recommend the perfect size and fit for each individual. This level of personalization goes beyond a simple size chart, fostering a sense of getting a product tailored specifically for your body and your adventures.

Product Recommendations: Patagonia leverages customer data and purchase history to provide personalized product recommendations both online and in-store. By analyzing customer preferences and behaviour, Patagonia can suggest relevant products that align with each customer's outdoor activities, climate preferences, and sustainability values.

Worn Wear Program: Patagonia's Worn Wear program allows customers to buy and sell used Patagonia gear. This program caters to the environmentally conscious customer who values sustainability and getting the most out of their gear. Additionally, Patagonia offers repair services, extending the life of their products and fostering a sense of responsible consumption. This personalization goes beyond just selling new products; it's about building a long-term relationship with customers and their gear. This initiative acknowledges that customers have different priorities and preferences when it comes to consumption - some prioritize sustainability and minimizing environmental impact over constantly purchasing new items.

Membership Programs: Patagonia's membership programs, such as the Patagonia Pro Program and Worn Wear, offer exclusive benefits, personalized rewards, and early access to product launches for members. These programs foster customer loyalty and engagement by providing personalized incentives and rewards based on each member's outdoor pursuits and interests.

Experience-Based Customization: Patagonia offers workshops and clinics on topics like backcountry skiing, fly fishing, and rock climbing. These experiences allow customers to connect with experts, learn new skills, and personalize their approach to outdoor pursuits.

Experience-based customization aligns with the ethos of personalization by allowing customers to tailor their outdoor experiences to their interests, skill levels, and preferences. By offering these workshops and clinics, Patagonia goes beyond merely selling products; they provide customers with the knowledge and resources needed to make the most of their outdoor adventures.

Moreover, these experiences foster a sense of community among outdoor enthusiasts, creating opportunities for like-minded individuals to come together, share experiences, and form lasting connections. As customers engage with Patagonia's workshops and clinics, they not only enhance their skills but also develop a deeper affinity for the brand, strengthening their emotional bond with Patagonia.

Patagonia Provisions: Patagonia Provisions offers a line of organic, high-performance food specifically designed for outdoor activities. This goes beyond simply selling apparel; it's about tailoring the entire outdoor experience. By offering personalized food options, Patagonia caters to its customers' specific needs and dietary preferences, fostering a sense of being a one-stop shop for all things adventure.

Patagonnia's focus on personalization fosters trust, strengthens the emotional connection, and positions Patagonia as more than just a brand; it becomes a trusted companion on every outdoor adventure.

In conclusion, personalization plays a crucial role in building emotional brands by delivering tailored experiences that resonate with customers on a personal level. By leveraging data and technology to understand customer preferences and needs, brands can create meaningful connections, enhance the customer experience, and foster long-term loyalty and advocacy. In the digital age, personalization is not just a competitive advantage but a strategic imperative for brands looking to differentiate themselves and forge deeper relationships with their audience.

* * *

7

Habit Forming Elements

The next factor crucial in building an emotional brand is habit formation. This entails incorporating elements into your product or service that encourage repeated use or engagement, ultimately leading to the formation of habits among consumers. Habit formation is powerful because it establishes a routine or behaviour pattern, fostering a sense of familiarity, comfort, and loyalty towards the brand.

One of the key principles underlying habit formation is the concept of "trigger-action-reward." This framework suggests that a trigger prompts a user to take action, which is then followed by a reward, reinforcing the behaviour and increasing the likelihood of its repetition. Successful brands understand this principle and strategically design their products or services to capitalize on it.

For example, social media platforms like Facebook and Instagram employ habit-forming elements to keep users coming back. The trigger may be a notification indicating new activity on a user's profile, prompting them to open the app (action). Upon opening the app, the user is rewarded with fresh content, likes, comments, or messages, satisfying their desire for social interaction (reward). Over time, this cycle of trigger-action-reward becomes ingrained in the user's routine, leading to habitual usage of the platform.

Similarly, brands in the fitness industry often leverage habit formation to encourage regular exercise and healthy lifestyle choices. Fitness apps and wearable devices use reminders, progress tracking, and rewards such as badges or virtual trophies to motivate users to work out consistently. By creating a sense of accomplishment and progress, these brands make exercising a habit rather than a chore.

Craving plays a critical role in habit formation. Brands aim to create triggers that elicit a craving or desire for the product or service. For example, the notification symbol on a social media app may trigger a craving for social interaction, prompting users to open the app to satisfy that craving.

Moreover, rewards in habit formation often involve variable rewards. Rather than providing the same reward every time a behaviour is performed, brands offer unpredictable or variable rewards, which are more effective in reinforcing habits. This variability keeps users engaged and motivated to continue engaging with the product or service.

For example, fitness apps may offer variable rewards such as badges, virtual trophies, or personalized insights based on the user's progress. These rewards provide a sense of accomplishment and satisfaction, encouraging users to continue their fitness routine in anticipation of the next reward.

Incorporating habit-forming elements into your product or service requires a deep understanding of your target audience's needs, preferences, and behaviours. By identifying triggers that prompt users to engage, designing seamless and intuitive experiences, and delivering meaningful rewards, brands can cultivate habits that strengthen their emotional connection with consumers.

Moreover, habit formation fosters long-term relationships with customers, as habits are often deeply ingrained and resistant to change. Once a consumer develops a habit around a particular brand or product, they are more likely to remain loyal and advocate for the brand, contributing to its success and sustainability in the marketplace.

In summary, habit formation is a powerful factor in building an emotional brand. By incorporating elements that encourage repeated use and engagement, brands can create lasting habits among consumers, leading to increased loyalty, retention, and advocacy.

Note: It's important to recognize that the subject of incorporating habit-forming elements into products or services requires in-depth study. Readers are encouraged to explore this topic further to gain a comprehensive understanding. However, it's essential to acknowledge that a detailed discussion on this matter is beyond the scope of this book. Additionally, not all products or services may be suitable for incorporating habit-forming elements. Therefore, it's advisable to assess whether your specific offering has the potential to include such elements before proceeding.

Apple iPod

Imagine the bustling streets of a city where people are immersed in their daily routines. Among the sea of commuters, a familiar sight emerges – the unmistakable white earbuds of an iPod. For millions around the world, the iPod isn't just a device; it's a companion that seamlessly integrates into their lives, becoming an essential part of their daily routines.

The design of the iPod is ingeniously crafted to form habits and become intertwined with the user's life. It begins with a simple trigger – perhaps the moment one steps out the door to embark on their daily commute or the instant they lace up their running shoes for a workout. This trigger prompts the action of reaching for the iPod, a sleek and familiar device that fits snugly in the palm of the hand.

With a click of the iconic circular wheel, the user navigates effortlessly through their music library, selecting the perfect playlist or album to accompany their journey. Whether it's the energizing beat of a favourite workout track or the soothing melody of a calming instrumental piece, the iPod caters to every mood and moment.

As the user becomes engrossed in their music, a routine is established. Day after day, the iPod accompanies them on their adventures, providing a soundtrack to their lives. It becomes a trusted companion during moments of solitude, a source of motivation during workouts, and a means of relaxation during downtime.

The allure of the iPod lies in its ability to provide variable rewards. With an extensive library of songs at their fingertips, users are constantly delighted by new discoveries and familiar favourites. Each shuffle brings the excitement of uncertainty – will it be a beloved classic or an exciting new track waiting to be heard?

But beyond the music itself, there's a deeper craving that the iPod satisfies. It's the longing for connection, emotion, and escape that music uniquely provides. Whether it's the euphoria of a catchy chorus, the nostalgia of a childhood anthem, or the comfort of a familiar melody, the iPod delivers an immersive experience that resonates with the soul.

Through its seamless integration into daily life, the iPod becomes more than just a device – it becomes a cherished part of the user's identity. It's a symbol of self-expression, personal taste, and individuality. From the morning commute to the late-night unwind, the iPod accompanies its users on their journey, forming habits and enriching their lives with the power of music.

Claude Hopkins and Pepsodent

In the early 1900s, Claude Hopkins faced a daunting task: selling Pepsodent toothpaste in an era when brushing teeth was not yet a widespread habit. Recognizing this challenge, Hopkins embarked on a mission to transform Pepsodent into more than just a product – he aimed to make it an integral part of people's daily routines.

Hopkins understood that to build a lasting connection with consumers, he needed to create a habit around brushing teeth, turning it into a ritual ingrained in people's lives. He realized that the success of Pepsodent depended not only on its effectiveness but also on its ability to become indispensable to consumers.

To achieve this, Hopkins set out to create a trigger that would prompt people to brush their teeth regularly. He introduced the concept of "the film," a cloudy residue that naturally forms on teeth overnight. Through clever marketing campaigns, Hopkins encouraged people to run their tongues over their teeth upon waking up – if they felt the film, it was a signal to brush with Pepsodent to remove it. This simple act served as a trigger, associating the sensation of the film with the need to use Pepsodent.

But Hopkins didn't stop there. He understood the importance of providing feedback to reinforce the habit. By introducing froth to Pepsodent, Hopkins provided users with a visual cue that brushing action was in progress, further solidifying the habit of using Pepsodent.

The promise of a reward also played a crucial role in Hopkins' strategy. He marketed Pepsodent as the key to a more beautiful smile – a reward that appealed to consumers' desire for enhanced appearance with minimal effort.

However, the true genius of Hopkins' approach lay in creating a craving for the product. Through the introduction of mint flavoring, Pepsodent provided users with a refreshing and invigorating sensation that left them craving the experience of brushing with Pepsodent again and again.

In essence, Hopkins's innovative use of habit-forming elements transformed Pepsodent from a mere toothpaste into an emotional brand that consumers trusted and relied on to care for their smiles. By tapping into the psychology of habit formation, Hopkins succeeded in making brushing with Pepsodent a daily ritual for millions of people worldwide.

Coca-Cola

Coca-Cola's journey to becoming an emotional brand is deeply intertwined with its strategic approach to building habits among consumers. From its inception, Coca-Cola recognized the importance of creating a habitual connection with its product, ensuring that it became an integral part of people's daily lives and routines.

The trigger for Coca-Cola's habit formation can be traced back to its iconic branding and marketing campaigns. Through clever advertising, Coca-Cola positioned itself as more than just a beverage; it became a symbol of happiness, togetherness, and refreshment. Whether through catchy jingles, heartwarming commercials, or captivating billboards, Coca-Cola consistently reinforced its presence in consumers' minds, creating a subconscious trigger to reach for a Coke in moments of joy, celebration, or relaxation.

Once the trigger was established, Coca-Cola focused on making the action of consuming its product as seamless and enjoyable as possible. Whether it was through convenient packaging, widespread availability, or innovative vending machines, Coca-Cola ensured that consumers could easily access and enjoy their favorite beverage whenever and wherever they desired.

The routine of drinking Coca-Cola became deeply ingrained in people's daily lives, evolving into a cherished ritual shared with friends, family, and colleagues. Whether it was sipping a Coke while watching a movie, sharing a cold bottle at a picnic, or grabbing a can from the office fridge, Coca-Cola became synonymous with moments of connection, joy, and relaxation.

To reinforce the habit, Coca-Cola offered variable rewards to consumers, ranging from the familiar taste and refreshing sensation of its beverages to the emotional satisfaction of being part of a global community united by a shared love for Coke. The crisp taste, effervescence, and sweetness of Coca-Cola provide instant gratification and pleasure, creating a positive association with the brand. Additionally, through catchy jingles, captivating advertisements, or memorable slogans like "Open Happiness," Coca-Cola triggers cravings for its products by appealing to consumers' desires for enjoyment, connection, and escapism.

To sum up, Coca-Cola's strategic approach to habit formation has enabled it to transcend being just a beverage and become an enduring symbol of happiness, unity, and positivity around the world.

In conclusion, incorporating habit-forming elements into a product or service is essential for building an emotional brand. By leveraging triggers, actions, and rewards, brands can cultivate habits among consumers, leading to increased loyalty and advocacy. However, it's important to note that this subject requires further study, and detailed discussion is beyond the scope of this book. Additionally, not all products or services may be suitable for incorporating habit-forming elements, so it's crucial to assess their potential before implementation.

* * *

8

Telling Stories

Telling stories is one of the most critical factors in building an emotional brand. Stories have a unique power to captivate, engage, and connect with customers on a deeply emotional level. When done effectively, storytelling can humanize a brand, convey its values and personality, and forge strong emotional bonds with consumers.

At its core, storytelling is about sharing experiences, beliefs, and aspirations in a compelling and relatable way. By crafting narratives that resonate with their target audience, brands can create a sense of authenticity that goes beyond mere advertising or promotion. Instead of focusing solely on product features or benefits, storytelling allows brands to communicate the deeper meaning behind their offerings and connect with consumers on a more profound level.

One of the key aspects of effective storytelling is authenticity. Today's consumers are savvy and discerning; they can quickly spot insincerity or manipulation. Therefore, it's essential for brands to tell genuine stories that reflect their values, mission, and commitment to their customers. Authentic storytelling builds trust and credibility, fostering a sense of loyalty and affinity among consumers.

Moreover, storytelling allows brands to differentiate themselves in a crowded marketplace. By sharing unique narratives that highlight their heritage, innovation, or social impact, brands can carve out a distinct identity and stand out from competitors. These stories become part of the brand's legacy, shaping how consumers perceive and interact with the brand over time.

Another crucial aspect of storytelling is emotional resonance. By tapping into universal themes such as love, courage, hope, and belonging, brands can evoke powerful emotions that resonate with audiences on a deeply personal level. Emotional storytelling creates a memorable and immersive experience, leaving a lasting impression on consumers and strengthening their emotional connection to the brand.

Furthermore, storytelling provides an opportunity for brands to engage with their audience in meaningful ways. Whether through social media, video content, or branded campaigns, brands can use storytelling to spark conversations, inspire action, and build a sense of community among their followers. By inviting consumers to be part of the story, brands can foster a sense of belonging and ownership, turning them into advocates and ambassadors for the brand.

In summary, Stories are the lifeblood of emotional branding. They have the power to connect with consumers on a deeper level, bypassing logic and tapping directly into emotions. Remember, people don't just buy products or services; they buy stories and the emotions they evoke. So, tell your brand story in a way that resonates with your audience and watch your emotional connection soar.

Incorporating Storytelling into Your Brand Strategy

1. **Customer Stories:** Sharing real-life experiences and testimonials from satisfied customers is a powerful way to showcase the positive impact your brand has on people's lives. By featuring authentic stories of how your product or service has solved problems, fulfilled needs, or brought joy to customers, you create relatable narratives that resonate with others facing similar challenges or aspirations.
2. **Brand Origin Story:** Every brand has a unique journey and story

behind its inception. Sharing your brand's origin story humanizes your company and allows consumers to connect with the passion, purpose, and values that drive your business. By highlighting the challenges, triumphs, and core beliefs that shaped your brand's identity, you create a compelling narrative that fosters emotional connections with your audience.

3. **Product Stories:** Instead of simply listing product features, focus on telling stories about how your product enhances the lives of its users. Highlight the emotional benefits and experiences that your product enables, such as feeling more confident, saving time, or creating cherished memories. By framing your product within the context of relatable human experiences, you make it more compelling and desirable to potential customers.

4. **Cause Marketing:** Partnering with a cause that aligns with your brand values allows you to make a positive impact in the world while also strengthening your brand's reputation and connection with consumers. By telling stories about the meaningful contributions your brand is making to support the cause, you demonstrate your commitment to social responsibility and inspire others to join you in making a difference.

5. **Emotional Archetypes:** Leveraging universal human emotions and archetypal themes in your storytelling can help you connect with a broad audience on a deeper level. By tapping into common themes such as overcoming challenges, achieving dreams, finding belonging, or experiencing love, you create narratives that resonate with the shared human experience. These emotional connections foster empathy, understanding, and affinity for your brand.

6. **Interactive Storytelling:** Explore interactive storytelling techniques that allow your audience to actively engage with your brand's narrative. Whether it's through quizzes, polls, interactive videos, or immersive experiences, interactive storytelling can captivate your audience's attention and deepen their emotional connection with your brand.

Incorporating these storytelling techniques into your brand strategy can help you create compelling narratives that resonate with your audience, build emotional connections, and differentiate your brand in the marketplace.

Strategies for Implementing Storytelling

1. **Create Compelling Content:** Utilize various content formats such as blogs, videos, podcasts, and social media posts to convey engaging narratives. Share behind-the-scenes insights, anecdotes, or success stories to offer your audience a deeper understanding of your brand.
2. **Use Visual Storytelling:** Incorporate visual elements like images, infographics, and videos to complement your brand narrative. Visuals have a powerful impact and can evoke emotions more effectively than text alone, enhancing the overall storytelling experience.
3. **Character Development:** Infuse your stories with well-developed characters that your audience can relate to and empathize with. Whether it's a customer overcoming a challenge, a founder pursuing their passion, or a beneficiary of your cause, compelling characters add depth and authenticity to your narratives.
4. **Conflict and Resolution:** Incorporate elements of conflict and resolution into your stories to create tension and keep your audience engaged. Highlight the obstacles or challenges your characters face, and demonstrate how your brand helps them overcome adversity and achieve their goals.
5. **Focus on Emotion:** Craft stories that resonate with your audience's emotions, values, and aspirations. Whether it's joy, inspiration, empathy, or nostalgia, tapping into these emotions can create a lasting connection with your brand.
6. **Stay Authentic:** Authenticity is paramount in storytelling. Be genuine and transparent in your communications, avoiding exaggeration or fabrication. Authentic stories resonate with audiences and build trust in your brand.
7. **Be Consistent:** Maintain a consistent brand voice and storytelling style across all marketing channels. Consistency reinforces your brand

identity and makes it easier for customers to recognize and engage with your stories.
8. **Engage Your Audience:** Foster interaction and engagement with your storytelling efforts by inviting feedback, asking questions, and creating opportunities for participation. User-generated content and interactive experiences can further enhance engagement and foster a sense of community around your brand.
9. **Adapt to Different Platforms:** Tailor your storytelling approach to suit the preferences and characteristics of different platforms. What works on social media may not be suitable for your website or email campaigns. Adapt your stories to fit the context and medium while maintaining a cohesive brand narrative.

The Underdogs: Swiped Mac

Apple's "Swiped" ad, also known as "The Underdogs: Swiped Mac," masterfully weaves a narrative that showcases the security features of Macbooks while captivating the audience with a thrilling storyline. The ad introduces viewers to a team of office workers, highlighting their reliance on laptops for work and setting the stage for the unfolding drama.

As the team collaborates on their top-secret project, disaster strikes when their leader, Bridget, has her MacBook stolen right outside their office. This sudden turn of events creates a sense of urgency and underscores the potential risks associated with losing valuable technology.

In a display of the MacBook's security features, Bridget receives an immediate notification on her phone alerting her to the theft and providing the latest location of her device. Determined to recover her MacBook, Bridget hails a taxi and uses the map on her phone to track the MacBook's movements.

Arriving at a pawn shop where the thieves have attempted to sell the MacBook, Bridget seamlessly pays the taxi fare using Apple Pay on her Apple Watch, showcasing the convenience and security of contactless payments.

Unfortunately, the thieves have already left since they could not unlock the Macbook, demonstrating the security feature. Undeterred, she continues her pursuit, now on a bicycle activated through an iPhone QR code.

As Bridget continues her pursuit on the bicycle, she receives a call from a concerned colleague, their voices echoing through her Apple Watch. However, with her focus solely on reclaiming the stolen MacBook, she reluctantly ignores the call, knowing her team understands the urgency of the situation. Meanwhile, another colleague swiftly checks his phone, utilizing the shared location feature to pinpoint Bridget's whereabouts. The seamless integration of Apple devices becomes evident as they all mobilize to assist Bridget, navigating their way to their parked car with the help of Siri's guidance.

While Bridget's team mobilizes, the thieves, unaware of the impending pursuit, seek to offload the stolen MacBook at a computer repair shop. However, their plans are thwarted when the shopkeeper refuses to purchase or use the MacBook due to its secure features, likening its security to that of Area 51. Frustrated and unable to sell the device, the thieves regroup over drinks, lamenting their failed attempts to profit from the stolen MacBook.

Desperate for a solution, the thieves turn to a tech-savvy acquaintance named Badger, known for his expertise in acquiring various items. As Bridget and her team race against time to catch up, Bridget takes advantage of her proximity to a colleague to remotely lock the MacBook using Touch ID, preventing unauthorized access to sensitive data. Although company policy mandates data wipe in case of a lost MacBook, Bridget hesitates, hopeful of retrieving the device intact.

As Bridget and her team converge on the counterfeit market, uncertainty looms over the MacBook's exact location amidst the bustling crowd. With a stroke of brilliance, Bridget's colleague suggests pinging the MacBook through their iPhone, prompting the device to emit a distinct ringing sound. The unexpected noise startles the thieves and Badger, compelling them to hastily dispose of the MacBook to evade detection.

Amidst the chaos of the chase, punctuated by moments of humour and tension, Bridget finally reaches the MacBook, reclaiming it from the clutches of the fleeing thieves. With a sense of relief and triumph, she enters the security code, securing the MacBook and bringing an end to the exhilarating pursuit. The screen fades to black, accompanied by the text "That's Mac Security at Work," encapsulating the narrative's message of resilience and the unwavering protection offered by Apple's security features.

Through compelling storytelling and relatable characters, Apple effectively communicates the empowering message of their products, guiding users through life's challenges while safeguarding their security and privacy. The ad seamlessly weaves advanced security features into the narrative, reinforcing Apple's dedication to enhancing user experiences and protecting digital lives.

Injecting humour into the tense situation, the ad captures the determination of Bridget and her team, fostering a strong connection with the audience. This blend of seriousness and humour makes the ad captivating and engaging, resonating with viewers on a personal level.

Furthermore, the ad subtly highlights the portability and seamless integration of MacBooks with other Apple devices, further solidifying their reputation as reliable tools for professionals. By eschewing technical jargon in favour of relatable scenarios, Apple effectively showcases how features like "Find My" and remote lock provide peace of mind for users.

In summary, Apple's "Swiped" ad masterfully employs storytelling to highlight the security features of MacBooks, creating an emotional connection through humor, teamwork, and a sense of relief.

Nike

Nike's storytelling ability has been a cornerstone of its brand identity and success, exemplified by its iconic "Just Do It" tagline and accompanying advertisements.

In 1987, Nike's ad agency created a TV spot celebrating the brand's role in founding the jogging craze. However, the initial ad focused more on showcasing Nike products rather than connecting with consumers on an emotional level. When previewed to a group of consumers, the ad met with silence, leaving Nike's founder, Phil Knight, upset.

Recognizing the need to shift the narrative, Nike and its ad agency revised the ad to highlight the emotional rewards of athleticism and the personal motivations of athletes. The revised ads featured athletes from various backgrounds speaking passionately about why they do what they do and the emotional satisfaction they derive from their pursuits. It is about their stories. This emphasis on emotional storytelling transformed the ad from a product-centric promotion to a powerful motivator, inspiring viewers to embrace the "Just Do It" mentality.

Rather than solely focusing on sneakers or product features, Nike's ads connected with viewers by tapping into universal desires for self-improvement, empowerment, and fulfilment. By showcasing athletes pursuing their passions and overcoming obstacles, Nike inspired audiences to take action and pursue their own dreams.

This simple yet powerful message has motivated countless individuals to step out of their comfort zones, push their limits, and pursue their goals with determination and resolve.

"Greatness" Campaign: During the 2012 London Olympics, Nike faced a challenge: unable to showcase its brand within the Olympic stadiums due to an exclusive deal with Adidas, they needed a creative strategy to stay relevant during the Games. Their solution was the "Greatness" campaign, a global initiative that shifted the narrative away from elite athletes to focus on everyday individuals pursuing personal excellence.

The campaign centred on storytelling, highlighting ordinary people striving for greatness in various locations worldwide. By showcasing relatable stories of perseverance, overcoming challenges, and achieving personal goals, Nike created an emotional connection with a broad audience. Whether it was runners in East London, dancers in Jamaica, or weightlifters in Ohio, the campaign resonated with people from diverse backgrounds and abilities.

Key to the campaign's success was its global appeal and use of social media. Hashtags like #findyourgreatness encouraged audience participation and fostered a sense of community around the concept of everyday greatness. The campaign's video ads, particularly the central "London" spot, showcased the diverse range of individuals pushing themselves to be their best, regardless of location or circumstance.

The impact of the "Greatness" campaign was profound. Despite not having an official Olympic sponsorship, Nike dominated the conversation with its relatable storytelling. By focusing on everyday people, they connected with audiences on a deeper level, inspiring feelings of empowerment and possibility. The campaign reinforced Nike's image as a brand that celebrates human potential, earning brand loyalty and solidifying its position as a beacon of inspiration worldwide.

Nike Air Jordan: Nike's storytelling prowess with the Air Jordan brand is legendary, demonstrating a masterclass in creating a narrative that transcends mere footwear. It all begins with the origin story, centring around a young, electrifying Michael Jordan, whose iconic presence on the court defied doubters and conventions alike. Nike astutely positioned him as a future legend even before he played a professional game, capitalizing on his potential to disrupt the status quo.

The narrative further unfolds with a David vs. Goliath theme as Nike, then a smaller brand, boldly backed a rookie player in the face of established giants like Converse. This underdog narrative struck a chord with fans who embraced the idea of challenging conventions. The Air Jordans weren't just shoes; they symbolized breaking barriers and pushing boundaries, epitomized by the banned "black and red" colourway that became a symbol of rebellion.

But beyond the product, Nike crafted an emotional connection with consumers. The Air Jordan story embodied aspiration, with Michael Jordan serving as a role model for young athletes striving for greatness. Limited releases and coveted styles added an aura of exclusivity, making owning a pair of Air Jordans a symbol of belonging to an elite group. The sneakers transcended basketball, becoming a cultural phenomenon worn by celebrities, musicians, and fashion icons alike.

Nike's storytelling techniques further amplified the brand's impact. Powerful advertising campaigns featuring MJ's electrifying dunks and catchy slogans like "Jumpman" and "Wings" cemented Air Jordans as the footwear of choice for those aspiring to achieve greatness. Strategic celebrity endorsements and collaborations with artists and designers added layers of collectability and storytelling to each shoe, enhancing its cultural relevance.

The result? The Air Jordan brand became more than just footwear; it became a cultural icon, a symbol of aspiration, and a legacy built on a captivating narrative. As the story continues to evolve with new releases and fan engagement initiatives, Nike ensures that the Air Jordan brand remains relevant and resonant across generations of sneaker enthusiasts.

TOMS Shoes

TOMS Shoes, founded by Blake Mycoskie, is a company that has woven its philanthropic mission into its brand narrative from the very beginning. The brand's "One for One" model, where for every pair of shoes purchased, a pair is donated to a child in need, has become an integral part of its storytelling approach.

Through its marketing campaigns, social media presence, and in-store experiences, TOMS Shoes has consistently shared stories that highlight the impact of its charitable initiatives. These stories go beyond mere product promotion and tap into the emotions of its customers by showcasing the real-life journeys and transformations of the individuals and communities they support.

One powerful example is the "One Day Without Shoes" campaign, where TOMS Shoes encourages people to go barefoot for a day to experience a life that many children face every day and raise awareness about the importance of providing shoes to those in need. This initiative not only raises funds but also creates a shared experience and emotional connection among customers and supporters, allowing them to become part of the brand's story.

TOMS Shoes has also leveraged the power of visual storytelling through its "Traveling Soles" campaign, which features captivating photography and videos that document the journeys of the donated shoes, showcasing the joy and gratitude on the faces of the children who receive them. These visually compelling stories evoke a sense of empathy and emotional resonance, fostering a deeper connection between the brand and its customers.

Furthermore, TOMS Shoes has incorporated storytelling into its retail experiences. In-store displays and product packaging often feature narratives and personal stories of the individuals and communities impacted by the brand's charitable initiatives. This immersive approach allows customers to connect with the brand's mission on a deeper level, fostering a sense of purpose and emotional investment in their purchase decisions.

By seamlessly weaving its philanthropic mission into its brand narrative and sharing compelling stories of impact, TOMS Shoes has cultivated a strong emotional bond with its customers. The brand's storytelling approach resonates with consumers who value purpose-driven brands and seek to make a positive impact on the world through their purchases.

Patagonia

Patagonia, a renowned outdoor clothing and gear company, has mastered the art of storytelling to build an emotional connection with its audience. Targeting a specific audience of people who value nature, adventure, and environmental responsibility, Patagonia's stories resonate deeply with those who share a passion for protecting the outdoors.

Through powerful visual narratives showcased in breathtaking documentaries and photography campaigns, Patagonia creates compelling stories that highlight the beauty of nature and the threats it faces. These stories urge viewers to take action, inspiring a sense of responsibility for preserving the natural world.

By evoking emotions like awe, wonder, and a profound sense of duty, Patagonia's storytelling creates a deeper connection with its audience. Viewers see Patagonia as more than just a brand; they perceive it as a beacon of environmental advocacy and ethical responsibility.

Patagonia's storytelling extends beyond selling products. The brand creates informative and engaging content, including blog posts, films, and social media campaigns, that educate and inspire its audience. Through these storytelling efforts, Patagonia reinforces its commitment to environmental activism and sustainable business practices, fostering a community of like-minded individuals dedicated to protecting the planet.

The Footprint Chronicles: Patagonia's "The Footprint Chronicles" is a groundbreaking storytelling initiative that plays a pivotal role in building the brand's emotional connection with its audience while highlighting its commitment to sustainability and transparency.

At its core, "The Footprint Chronicles" serves as a window into the environmental impact of the fashion industry, offering consumers an inside look at Patagonia's supply chain and the journey of its products from conception to delivery. Through a series of engaging and informative documentaries, Patagonia shines a light on the ecological footprint associated with the production, transportation, and disposal of its garments.

By providing a transparent view of its operations and the challenges inherent in achieving sustainability, Patagonia fosters trust and authenticity with its audience. Consumers are not only informed about the environmental impact of their purchasing decisions but also empowered to make more conscious choices about the products they buy.

"The Footprint Chronicles" also humanizes the brand by showcasing the people behind the products, from factory workers to designers, highlighting their dedication to creating high-quality and eco-friendly apparel. This storytelling approach creates a sense of empathy and connection with Patagonia's audience, who see the brand as more than just a clothing manufacturer but as a group of individuals united by a common purpose.

Moreover, "The Footprint Chronicles" serves as a call to action, inspiring viewers to take steps towards reducing their own environmental footprint and advocating for positive change within the fashion industry. By raising awareness and encouraging collective action, Patagonia strengthens its emotional bond with its audience, positioning itself as a catalyst for environmental stewardship and social responsibility.

Don't Buy This Jacket: This is one of Patagonia's most iconic storytelling campaigns. At its core, the campaign challenges the prevailing consumerist mindset and urges people to reconsider their purchasing habits in favour of mindful consumption and environmental stewardship. The bold and provocative message, "Don't Buy This Jacket," featured prominently in print and digital advertisements, caught the attention of consumers and sparked a conversation about the true cost of consumerism.

The campaign was centred around a full-page advertisement in The New York Times on Black Friday, one of the busiest shopping days of the year. Instead of promoting rampant consumerism and urging people to buy more, Patagonia took a bold stance by encouraging consumers to think twice before making a purchase, particularly for items they didn't truly need.

The emotional impact of the campaign lies in its authenticity and transparency. By acknowledging the environmental impact of its own products and urging consumers to consume less, Patagonia demonstrated a commitment to its values of sustainability and responsible business practices. This authenticity resonated with consumers, who appreciated the brand's honesty and integrity.

Moreover, the campaign leveraged storytelling to convey a powerful message about the consequences of overconsumption and the importance of making informed choices. Through compelling visuals and compelling narratives, Patagonia highlighted the environmental footprint of its products and encouraged consumers to consider the true cost of their purchases on the planet.

Ultimately, the "Don't Buy This Jacket" campaign succeeded in creating a meaningful dialogue around sustainability and consumerism, inspiring individuals to rethink their relationship with material possessions and adopt a more conscious approach to consumption.

Through authentic storytelling and a commitment to ethical business practices, Patagonia continues to inspire and engage its audience, driving positive change and making a lasting impact on both the fashion industry and the planet.

Product Story—Febreze

In Charles Duhigg's book "The Power Of Habit," he shares a captivating product story that revolves around Laura, an independent woman in her late twenties living in Phoenix. Laura works as a park ranger, where her job involves trapping skunks—a task that often leaves her covered in their pungent spray.

Despite her attractiveness and intelligence, Laura's love life remains stagnant. The overpowering smell of skunk that permeates her home, clothing, and belongings acts as a barrier to forming meaningful connections. Laura's romantic prospects are hindered by the fear of potential partners being repelled by the odour.

Laura's attempts to overcome this obstacle prove futile as she tries various remedies, from special soaps to expensive carpet cleaning machines, all to no avail. Her desperation grows as she longs for a solution to reclaim her social life and alleviate her loneliness.

Enter Febreze—a product that offers a glimmer of hope for Laura. Sceptical but willing to try anything, Laura sprays Febreze on every surface tainted by the skunk smell. To her amazement, the odour disappears, leaving her home fresh and inviting. Excited by the transformation, Laura invites her friends over, who confirm that they can no longer detect the skunk odour.

For Laura, the impact of Febreze extends far beyond eliminating a foul smell—it revitalizes her confidence, restores her social life, and brings her closer to achieving her dreams of starting a family. Febreze becomes more than just a household product; it becomes a symbol of hope and transformation in Laura's life.

The compelling narrative of Laura and Febreze serves as a poignant example of how a brand can tell a captivating product story to deeply connect with its audience.

Warby Parker

Warby Parker's origin story is rooted in a frustration familiar to many: the high cost of prescription eyewear and the lack of affordable options in the market. The company's founders—Neil Blumenthal, Andrew Hunt, David Gilboa, and Jeffrey Raider—experienced this problem firsthand and were inspired to take action. They envisioned a new kind of eyewear company, one that would disrupt the industry by offering stylish, high-quality glasses at a fraction of the price of traditional retailers.

Rather than keeping this frustration to themselves, the founders leveraged it as the cornerstone of their brand narrative. They shared their personal experiences and motivations openly, articulating their vision for change and their commitment to addressing a longstanding issue in the eyewear market. By doing so, they humanized the brand and made it relatable to a wide audience who could empathize with their struggles and aspirations.

Before even unveiling their products or marketing their benefits, the founders strategically prioritized storytelling. They recognized the power of narrative in capturing attention, building anticipation, and fostering emotional connections with consumers. Everywhere they went—whether it was through media interviews, social media channels, or grassroots marketing efforts—they shared the Warby Parker story. This relentless focus on storytelling helped to generate buzz, intrigue, and curiosity among potential customers.

Central to Warby Parker's origin story was its commitment to social impact. The founders believed that access to affordable eyewear was not just a business opportunity but also a social responsibility. They implemented the "Buy a Pair, Give a Pair" program, pledging to donate a pair of glasses to someone in need for every pair sold. This philanthropic initiative not only reflected Warby Parker's values but also resonated deeply with consumers who sought to support businesses with a purpose.

By aligning their brand narrative with their values and mission, the founders effectively leveraged storytelling to connect with consumers on an emotional level. The Warby Parker story—rooted in frustration, fueled by innovation, and guided by a commitment to social impact—became a rallying cry for those seeking authenticity, affordability, and social responsibility in the products they purchased.

Real Beauty Sketches

One example of a customer story used by a brand to promote its product is the "Real Beauty Sketches" campaign by Dove.

In this campaign, Dove sought to challenge societal norms and celebrate the natural beauty of women of all ages, shapes, and sizes. Instead of relying on traditional advertising tactics, Dove chose to tell the stories of real women and their perceptions of their own beauty.

The campaign involved an experiment where women were asked to describe their appearance to a forensic sketch artist, who then created two sketches—one based on the women's descriptions of themselves and another based on descriptions provided by strangers who had briefly met the women.

The results of the experiment were striking. The sketches based on strangers' descriptions consistently portrayed the women as more attractive and happier than the sketches based on the women's self-descriptions. This stark contrast highlighted the gap between how women perceive themselves and how others perceive them.

Through powerful video testimonials and interviews with the participants, Dove shared the emotional journey of these women as they grappled with their self-image and learned to embrace their natural beauty. The campaign aimed to inspire women to reassess their own perceptions of beauty and recognize their inherent worth and uniqueness.

By sharing real stories of women confronting their insecurities and embracing their true selves, Dove created a deeply emotional and relatable narrative that resonated with audiences worldwide. The campaign sparked conversations about beauty standards, self-esteem, and body positivity, ultimately reinforcing Dove's commitment to promoting real beauty and empowering women to feel confident in their own skin.

The "Real Beauty Sketches" campaign exemplifies the power of storytelling to connect with consumers on a profound emotional level and drive meaningful change in societal perceptions of beauty.

In conclusion, storytelling emerges as a critical factor in building an emotional brand. Through narratives that resonate with audiences on a personal level, brands can forge deep connections, evoke emotions, and foster loyalty. By weaving compelling stories that highlight their values, mission, and the impact of their products or services, companies can create a lasting impression that transcends mere transactions. Ultimately, storytelling serves as a powerful tool for brands to differentiate themselves in a crowded marketplace, leaving a memorable and emotional imprint on their audience.

* * *

9

Speak in the Consumer's Language

The next crucial factor in building an emotional brand is speaking in the consumer's language. This means understanding their needs, desires, and preferences on a deep level and tailoring your brand messaging accordingly. Rather than bombarding consumers with technical jargon or generic marketing speak, brands need to communicate in a way that resonates with their audience on a personal and emotional level.

One effective way to speak in the consumer's language is to focus on the benefits and outcomes of your product or service rather than just its features. Instead of simply listing specifications or capabilities, highlight how your offering solves a problem, fulfills a need, or enhances the consumer's life in some way.

For example, if you're selling a fitness tracker, don't just talk about its advanced sensors and tracking capabilities. Instead, emphasize how it helps users stay motivated, track their progress, and achieve their fitness goals. By framing the product in terms of the benefits it provides—such as improved health, increased energy, and a sense of accomplishment—you speak directly to the consumer's desires and aspirations.

Furthermore, it's essential to use language that resonates with your target audience's values, interests, and lifestyle. Whether you're addressing millennials, baby boomers, outdoor enthusiasts, or urban dwellers, tailor your messaging to speak to their unique needs and preferences. This might involve using colloquial language, cultural references, or imagery that reflects their demographic or psychographic profile.

In addition to product messaging, brands can also connect with consumers on a deeper level by sharing stories, testimonials, and user-generated content that showcase real-life experiences and emotions. Authenticity is key here—consumers can quickly spot insincerity, so it's essential to speak from a place of genuine understanding and empathy.

Overall, speaking in the consumer's language is about fostering a sense of connection, understanding, and trust. By communicating in a way that resonates with their needs, desires, and values, brands can build stronger emotional connections with their audience and differentiate themselves in a crowded marketplace.

Example

Skincare Brand X understands that millennials are not just looking for effective skincare products but also ones that align with their values of sustainability and eco-friendliness. Instead of bombarding consumers with complex scientific terms, the brand's messaging focuses on the following:

a. Benefit-Oriented Messaging: Instead of emphasizing the ingredients used in their products, the brand highlights the benefits, such as promoting healthy, radiant skin, reducing the appearance of fine lines, and providing protection from environmental stressors. They communicate how their products contribute to a holistic skincare routine that nurtures the skin and boosts confidence.

b. Environmental Responsibility: The brand speaks to millennials' concerns about environmental sustainability by highlighting their commitment to eco-friendly practices. They discuss their use of recyclable packaging, cruelty-free ingredients, and sustainable sourcing methods. Messaging emphasizes how choosing their products aligns with the consumer's values of reducing their environmental footprint and supporting ethical practices.

c. Lifestyle Alignment: Recognizing that millennials lead busy, on-the-go lifestyles, the brand positions its products as convenient and easy to incorporate into daily routines. They emphasize features like quick absorption, lightweight textures, and multi-functional formulas. Messaging resonates with millennials' desire for products that fit seamlessly into their active lifestyles, whether they're at work, at the gym, or travelling.

By speaking in the consumer's language, this skincare brand effectively connects with environmentally conscious millennials on a deeper level. They address their concerns, values, and lifestyle preferences, ultimately building stronger emotional connections and fostering brand loyalty.

Pampers

In 1997, Pampers, a brand known for its superior dryness technology, found itself in a sticky situation. Sales were sluggish, and their grip on the diaper market was loosening to their competitor, Huggies. Despite having a demonstrably drier product, Pampers was failing to connect with new parents.

Through user research, Pampers discovered a crucial truth – dryness, while important, wasn't the primary concern for sleep-deprived parents. Their anxieties ran deeper, focused on their baby's overall health and development. This realization sparked a transformation in Pampers' approach.

They pivoted their communication strategy, moving away from dry claims and towards the emotional core of parenthood – a baby's well-being. Pampers began speaking the language of new parents, highlighting how their diapers could contribute to a baby's sound sleep, a critical factor for healthy development. This emotional connection resonated deeply. Parents saw Pampers not just as a diaper brand but as a partner in their child's journey.

The storytelling didn't stop there. Pampers understood that a baby's needs change rapidly. They introduced targeted product categories like Swaddlers for the delicate needs of newborns, Cruisers for active toddlers, and Pull-Ups to support toilet training. This spoke volumes about Pampers' commitment to understanding the various stages of development, offering a solution for every gurgle and giggle.

By focusing on the emotional needs of parents and offering targeted products, Pampers reconnected with its audience. They shifted from selling a product to offering peace of mind, a good night's sleep for both baby and parent and ultimately, a well-rested foundation for a healthy, thriving child.

Snickers

Snickers was stuck in a sugar rut. By the late 1990s, its chocolate bars sat on shelves, failing to connect with its target audience—young men. Sure, they satisfied a craving, but they lacked the spark to truly resonate. Sales mirrored this lacklustre connection, remaining stubbornly stagnant.

A shift in perspective, however, was about to change the game. Through research, Snickers unearthed a hidden gem – their core audience often found themselves in a particular state: a blend of hunger and frustration they dubbed "hanger" (hunger anger). This revelation became the key that unlocked a new way of speaking to their customers.

Gone were the generic candy bar commercials. Snickers launched a now-legendary campaign built entirely around the concept of "hanger." Hilarious ads showcased everyday situations where men turned into grumpy, irrational versions of themselves due to low blood sugar. For example, their "You're Not You When You're Hungry" campaign featured humorous commercials depicting people acting out of character due to hunger, only to return to normal after eating a Snickers bar. This campaign effectively communicated the brand's message while entertaining and engaging consumers. These relatable scenarios struck a chord with the target audience.

The language resonated deeply. It wasn't just about chocolate; it was about the emotional state their audience faced – the frustration and annoyance caused by hunger. Snickers spoke their language, using humour and authenticity to create a sense of camaraderie. They weren't just selling a treat; they were offering a solution to "hanger" – a quick fix to restore good mood and energy.

The "You're Not You When You're Hungry" campaign was a runaway success. It did more than just boost sales (which skyrocketed, solidifying Snickers' leadership in the chocolate bar market). It repositioned the brand. Snickers transformed from a simple candy bar into a solution for a relatable problem, a lifeline in the throes of hanger-induced meltdowns. By understanding their audience's deeper frustrations and creating a language around them, Snickers forged a powerful emotional connection, proving that sometimes, the sweetest success comes from speaking the right language.

Always (Pads & Liners)

Always, a leading brand in feminine hygiene products faced the challenge of addressing the discomfort and social stigma associated with menstruation. Their target audience, women of all ages experiencing menstruation, desired more than just a product—they sought confidence, comfort, and freedom during their periods. To speak the consumer's language effectively, Always focused on highlighting the emotional and social benefits of their pads and liners rather than technical features.

Their campaigns, such as "Like a Girl" and "#EndPeriodStigma," tackled social issues surrounding menstruation, encouraging women to embrace their bodies and challenge stereotypes. Utilizing relatable language and imagery, Always created authentic and genuine messaging that resonated with their audience. They didn't shy away from using the word "period" and addressed real issues faced by women, fostering a sense of trust and connection.

By speaking directly to the experiences of menstruating women and focusing on values and interests that mattered to them, Always built a strong emotional connection with their audience. Their approach went beyond selling products; it positioned Always as a brand that supports and empowers women during their periods, ultimately enhancing brand loyalty and advocacy.

Duolingo

Imagine wanting to learn a new language but feeling overwhelmed by textbooks and grammar drills. That's the frustration Duolingo speaks to. They ditch the technical jargon and instead talk about "unlocking conversations" and "building the confidence to order food in Italian." Rather than highlighting grammar rules or vocabulary lists, Duolingo's messaging revolves around how learning a new language can open doors to new opportunities, enhance cognitive skills, and connect people from different cultures. Their message is clear: learning a language should be fun, not frustrating.

Duolingo knows its audience. They're not targeting language scholars; they're reaching out to everyday people who yearn to connect with new cultures or boost their careers. Their marketing is lighthearted and relatable, using humour for younger audiences and highlighting career advancement for professionals.

This isn't a one-size-fits-all approach. Duolingo offers a diverse range of languages and caters to different learning styles. Leaderboards and forums create a sense of community, while user testimonials showcase real-life success stories. It's all about authenticity – the friendly green owl Duo is a mascot you can't help but trust.

In conclusion, speaking in the consumer's language is not just about conveying information but about building connections. By focusing on the benefits rather than just features, tailoring messaging to align with values and lifestyle, and incorporating authentic storytelling, brands can create deeper emotional bonds with their audience. This fosters trust, loyalty, and a stronger brand identity, ultimately setting them apart in a competitive market landscape.

* * *

10

Authentic Messaging

Authentic messaging involves communicating with honesty, transparency, and sincerity, aligning your brand's values with your actions, and establishing genuine connections with your audience.

Key components of authentic messaging include:

1. **Transparency:** Authentic messaging involves being open and transparent with the audience about the brand's practices, values, and offerings. This includes acknowledging any shortcomings or mistakes and being upfront about how the brand operates.
2. **Alignment with Values:** Ensuring your messaging reflects your brand's core beliefs. If you promote sustainability, your actions and communication should consistently uphold that commitment.
3. **Genuine Intentions:** Authentic messaging is driven by genuine intentions to connect with the audience and meet their needs. It focuses on building meaningful relationships rather than solely promoting products or services.
4. **Amplifying Customer Voices:** Showcasing testimonials, reviews, and user-generated content that depict genuine experiences with your brand. This resonates more than meticulously crafted ads.
5. **Telling real stories:** Sharing genuine narratives, experiences, and behind-the-scenes glimpses that provide an authentic look into your

brand, its people, and its values.
6. **Using relatable language:** Communicating in a down-to-earth, conversational tone that feels natural and approachable rather than overly polished or salesy.
7. **Showcasing real people:** Featuring real employees, customers, or community members in your messaging rather than relying solely on staged or idealized depictions.
8. **Admitting imperfections:** Being transparent about challenges, mistakes, or areas for improvement, rather than portraying an unrealistic level of perfection.
9. **Focus on People:** Centering your messaging on the human experiences and stories associated with your brand. This fosters deeper connections than simply highlighting product features.
10. **Consistency:** Authentic messaging requires consistency across all communication channels and touchpoints. The brand's messaging should align with its actions and behaviours to avoid discrepancies and maintain trust with the audience.

Here's why authentic messaging is essential and how it contributes to building an emotional brand:

1. **Trust and Credibility:** Authentic messaging builds trust with your audience. When you communicate honestly and transparently, consumers are more likely to believe in your brand and perceive you as credible. Trust is the foundation of any successful relationship, and by being authentic in your messaging, you establish a solid foundation of trust with your audience.
2. **Human Connection:** Authentic messaging allows you to connect with your audience on a human level. By sharing real stories, experiences, and emotions, you create relatable content that resonates with people's lives. When consumers see themselves reflected in your brand's messaging, they feel understood, valued, and more likely to develop an emotional

connection with your brand.

3. **Differentiation:** In a crowded marketplace, authenticity sets your brand apart from the competition. Consumers are inundated with marketing messages every day, but authentic messaging stands out because it feels genuine and sincere. When your brand communicates with authenticity, you differentiate yourself from brands that rely on gimmicks or false promises, making it easier for consumers to choose you over competitors.

4. **Brand Loyalty:** Authentic messaging fosters loyalty among your audience. When consumers feel a genuine connection with your brand, they are more likely to become repeat customers and brand advocates. Authenticity creates a sense of loyalty because consumers trust that your brand will deliver on its promises and continue to act in their best interests.

5. **Emotional Engagement:** Authentic messaging evokes emotions and creates memorable experiences for your audience. When you tell compelling stories, share authentic content, and engage with consumers on a personal level, you trigger emotional responses that strengthen their connection to your brand. Emotions play a powerful role in decision-making, and by appealing to consumers' emotions, you create lasting impressions that drive loyalty and advocacy.

6. **Long-Term Relationships:** Authentic messaging builds long-term relationships with your audience. By consistently delivering authentic content and experiences, you cultivate a loyal following that remains engaged with your brand over time. These long-term relationships are invaluable for sustaining your brand's success and weathering challenges that may arise.

Ultimately, authenticity lies in focusing on people rather than products. By centring your messaging around the human experiences and stories associated with your brand, you can forge deeper connections with your audience and establish a genuine and lasting rapport.

Cheerios

Cheerios has mastered the art of authentic messaging, cultivating a strong emotional bond with consumers by tapping into the universal experiences and joys of family life. The brand's advertising campaigns depict heartwarming, relatable moments of parents and children sharing breakfast together, instantly resonating with viewers on an emotional level.

Beyond traditional advertising, Cheerios amplifies the voices and experiences of real families through user-generated content shared across its social media channels. Photos and stories of families enjoying Cheerios together foster an authentic connection by showcasing the brand's presence in the lives of its consumers.

Cheerios has demonstrated a commitment to inclusivity and celebrating all types of families. The 2014 "Love" campaign featured an interracial family enjoying Cheerios, triggering some negative reactions initially. However, Cheerios stood firm, reinforcing its message of inclusivity and reinforcing its authentic depiction of the modern family – a stance that resonated emotionally with many viewers.

The brand has also leveraged authentic messaging to spread positivity and foster emotional connections through simple acts of kindness. The "Good Goes Round" campaign highlighted real stories of people performing good deeds within their communities, reinforcing Cheerios' message of spreading joy and bringing people together.

Cheerios' authentic messaging extends beyond just its campaigns. The brand has been transparent about the simple, wholesome ingredients in its products, emphasizing phrases like "Whole Grain Oats" and "No artificial flavours or colours" to build trust and openness with consumers. This transparency aligns with Cheerios' core values of simplicity, wholesomeness, and family-centricity, which are consistently promoted through its brand identity and messaging.

The brand's genuine intentions shine through, as its messaging aims to connect with families and promote shared moments over a healthy breakfast rather than solely focusing on product promotion. Cheerios communicates in a warm, down-to-earth tone that resonates with its family-oriented audience, avoiding corporate jargon or overly polished language in favour of a conversational and approachable style.

Cheerios' commercials and advertisements feature real families, fostering a genuine connection and sense of relatability by authentically representing its consumers. While promoting a positive brand image, Cheerios has also acknowledged and addressed concerns or controversies related to its advertising campaigns, contributing to its authentic messaging through transparency and a willingness to address challenges.

At its core, Cheerios' messaging centres on the human experiences and emotional connections associated with its brand, such as shared family moments and cherished traditions. This focus on people fosters deeper emotional bonds than simply highlighting product features.

Patagonia

Patagonia wasn't built on a foundation of marketing speak. It was born from a love of exploration and a deep respect for the wild places we explore. This authenticity, woven into the very fabric of their brand, is what makes their messaging resonate so deeply.

They don't just sell clothes; they sell a philosophy. Their message isn't about the latest trends; it's about protecting the playgrounds we wear their gear in. They consistently walk the walk, using recycled materials, encouraging gear repair, and actively supporting environmental causes. This isn't some fleeting marketing campaign; it's a core tenet that informs everything they do.

Across its marketing campaigns, social media platforms, and corporate communications, Patagonia boldly addresses pressing environmental issues such as climate change, pollution, and habitat destruction. Rather than shying away from uncomfortable truths, the company confronts them head-on, sparking meaningful conversations and inspiring action.

Take their "Worn Wear" campaign, for example. It's not just about selling used Patagonia products; it's about the stories those products hold. They celebrate the adventures each rip and tear represents, encouraging customers to keep their gear in use for as long as possible. This focus on sustainability and extending the life cycle of their products speaks volumes about Patagonia's commitment to minimizing their environmental footprint.

Transparency is another pillar of their authenticity. They're not afraid to acknowledge the challenges of running a sustainable business. They share their struggles and victories, fostering a sense of trust with their customers. This vulnerability allows them to connect with environmentally conscious consumers who appreciate Patagonia's genuine efforts to make a difference. The company also openly shares insights into its supply chain, manufacturing processes, and environmental impact, fostering trust and credibility among consumers. By laying bare its operations, Patagonia demonstrates a commitment to accountability and integrity.

Patagonia's message isn't just about selling you a jacket; it's about inviting you to join a movement. They inspire people to explore the natural world responsibly, to value quality over quantity, and to fight for the preservation of wild places. This emotional connection, built on a foundation of authenticity and shared values, is what makes Patagonia a brand that resonates far beyond the retail shelf.

Always(Pads and Liners)

When it started, Always brand was in a sticky situation. Periods were a fact of life, yet their products felt sterile, existing in a world of hushed tones and awkward glances. They were seen as purely functional, failing to connect with the emotional realities of menstruation.

Always knew they had to break free from this cycle. They realized their messaging needed to go beyond product benefits and delve into the social and emotional aspects of periods. This shift towards authentic messaging unfolded in a few key ways:

First came the iconic "Like a Girl" campaign. This powerful social experiment challenged the negative connotations associated with doing things "like a girl." It resonated deeply with women who had experienced feeling judged for their strength, boldness, or athleticism simply because they were girls. This wasn't about selling pads; it was about sparking a conversation, dismantling societal expectations, and empowering young women to embrace who they are.

Always didn't stop there. They launched the #EndPeriodStigma movement, actively promoting open and honest conversations about menstruation. Partnering with influencers and organizations, they aimed to normalize periods and break down the stigma surrounding them. This focus on social change positioned Always as a brand that understood these challenges and supported women, not just with products, but with a voice.

Finally, Always embraced real stories. Their advertising featured real women of all backgrounds and body types, showcasing the diverse experiences of menstruation. They celebrated the strength and resilience of women, normalizing periods and fostering a sense of authenticity. This focus on real people wasn't just relatable; it built trust and a connection that transcended product features.

The impact was undeniable. Always' authentic messaging addressed the emotional and social anxieties women face during menstruation. This resonated deeply, building a strong emotional connection with their audience. They weren't just selling a product; they were shifting the conversation, normalizing periods, and fostering a sense of empowerment. By prioritizing authenticity and social impact, Always cultivated a loyal customer base who appreciated their commitment to positive change. This journey transformed Always from a period product brand into a brand that stands by women, a brand that champions their journeys and celebrates their strength, period.

Dollar Shave Club

Dollar Shave Club burst onto the scene with an unconventional and irreverent marketing approach that immediately captured attention for its authenticity. The brand's viral launch video featured the founder, Michael Dubin, delivering a humorous and profanity-laced monologue about the company's mission to provide affordable razors without the gimmicks of traditional shaving companies.

This raw, unfiltered messaging style established Dollar Shave Club's authentic voice from the outset. They weren't afraid to laugh at themselves, either. A touch of self-deprecation in their marketing made them instantly relatable. They poked fun at the industry and themselves, fostering a sense of camaraderie with their audience. This humour disarmed potential customers and felt like a breath of fresh air compared to the usual industry posturing.

Dollar Shave Club's messaging emphasized simplicity, transparency, and accessibility. The brand didn't try to convince you their razors were the pinnacle of shaving technology (although they did claim they were "good enough"). They focused on what truly mattered: value. High-quality blades, delivered straight to your doorstep, all at a fraction of the cost of the big brands. This resonated with a generation tired of feeling scammed by exaggerated claims and unnecessary markups.

Beyond its marketing campaigns, Dollar Shave Club's commitment to authenticity extended to its product offerings and customer experience. The brand's subscription model and minimalist product lineup reflected a focus on simplicity and convenience, catering to the needs of consumers who valued no-frills solutions.

Dollar Shave Club also leveraged user-generated content and customer reviews to amplify the voices of its loyal subscribers. By sharing real experiences and testimonials, the brand reinforced its authentic messaging and fostered a genuine connection with its audience.

Additionally, Dollar Shave Club embraced transparency in addressing challenges and product issues. When faced with quality concerns or supply chain disruptions, the brand was upfront with its customers, acknowledging the problems and outlining steps to address them. This willingness to admit imperfections and prioritize open communication contributed to the brand's authentic messaging and built trust with its customer base.

By embracing a refreshingly honest, relatable, and self-deprecating tone, emphasizing simplicity, transparency, and value, and amplifying customer voices, Dollar Shave Club cultivated an emotional brand connection with its audience. They positioned themselves as a genuine and trustworthy alternative in the shaving industry, fostering a sense of camaraderie with a generation tired of feeling scammed.

Chobani Yogurt

Chobani's brand story is rooted in authenticity, stemming from the personal journey of its founder, Hamdi Ulukaya. As a Kurdish immigrant from Turkey, Ulukaya started Chobani with the goal of making high-quality, nutritious yogurt accessible to all Americans, using authentic recipes and traditional methods.

This authentic origin story shapes Chobani's messaging, which emphasizes the company's commitment to using only natural ingredients and time-honoured techniques. The brand's "Nothing But Good" tagline encapsulates this promise, resonating with consumers seeking genuine, wholesome products.

Chobani's marketing campaigns often feature real employees, farmers, and community members, showcasing the brand's deep ties to its roots and the people behind its products. These authentic stories and faces humanize the brand, fostering emotional connections with consumers who value transparency and real-life narratives.

In addition to highlighting its authentic production methods and ingredients, Chobani's messaging also centres around its philanthropic initiatives and commitment to giving back. The brand has been transparent about its efforts to support local communities, provide food to those in need, and promote sustainable farming practices. This alignment of messaging with socially responsible values resonates with consumers seeking purpose-driven brands.

Chobani's approach to addressing challenges and controversies also reflects its authentic messaging. When faced with issues, such as a product recall or workplace concerns, the brand has been open and transparent in communicating with its customers and stakeholders, acknowledging the problems and outlining steps to address them. This willingness to embrace transparency and accountability contributes to the brand's authentic identity.

Furthermore, Chobani actively encourages and amplifies the voices of its loyal consumers through user-generated content and online communities. By sharing real stories and experiences from its customers, the brand reinforces its authentic connection with its audience and fosters a sense of community around its products.

Chobani's authentic messaging extends beyond just its marketing campaigns. The brand's packaging and product offerings reflect its commitment to simplicity and naturalness, with clean labels, minimal ingredients, and a focus on traditional yogurt varieties.

The brand's authentic messaging resonates with growing consumer demand for wholesome, trustworthy products and companies that prioritize authenticity over marketing gimmicks.

In conclusion, authenticity has become a powerful way for brands to forge emotional connections with consumers in today's crowded marketplace. Authentic messaging involves transparency, telling real stories, amplifying customer voices, using relatable language, showcasing real people, admitting imperfections, and consistency across touchpoints.

In an era of scepticism towards traditional marketing, authentic messaging allows brands to establish lasting emotional bonds with audiences craving authenticity and purpose-driven experiences. By embracing vulnerability and staying true to core values, brands can cultivate loyalty and advocacy through genuine connections.

* * *

11

Building Relationships with Customers

Celia stepped through the doors of Parkview Pet Supply and was instantly transported back to her childhood. The unmistakable scents of dog treats and wood shavings, the cacophony of bird chirps and fish tank bubblers - it all flooded her with a wave of warm nostalgia. This was the same family-owned pet store her parents had brought her to pick out each new addition to their household menagerie when she was a little girl.

"Well, hey there, Miss Celia!" Dennis, the jovial owner, emerged from the aisles with a friendly grin. "I was just taking inventory on the new line of natural dog foods that came in. Let me grab you a sample pack for Bailey!"

Celia felt a surprised smile spread across her face. She hadn't even mentioned bringing home treats for her lab mix yet. But of course, Dennis remembered - he always did. He also knew Bailey's name, breed, latest antics, and Celia's preferred brands and flavors like the back of his hand.

As Dennis rang up her purchase, chatting amiably about Celia's upcoming beach vacation with Bailey, she realized how remarkable this level of personalized attention was. Despite running a busy small business, Dennis made every customer feel special and valued, like part of the Parkview family.

In the capable hands of the Parkview staff, picking up pet supplies was so much more than just another errand. It was an experience shaped by caring individuals who seamlessly blended expertise, attention to detail, and good old-fashioned personal touch. These details kept Celia coming back year after year, rehashing fond childhood memories with each visit.

The undeniable truth was Celia's loyalty to Parkview Pet Supply extended far beyond their products.

Companies today often view customers through a purely transactional lens - a means to an end, numbers on a spreadsheet. However, the bonds between a business and its customers can be so much deeper than that. When a brand takes the time to form real relationships, to create positive experiences and memories, it begins to earn a special place in people's lives. An emotional connection is forged that inspires fierce loyalty, repeat business, and advocacy. Customers don't just choose that business for its products or services - they choose it for how it makes them feel...

> In today's competitive landscape, consumers crave connection, and brands that excel at building relationships with their customers are the ones that thrive.

Here are some key strategies for building strong relationships with customers:

1. **Get Personal:** Take the time to really get to know your customers - their names, preferences, interests, and needs. Use this information to personalize your interactions and offerings. Personalized attention makes customers feel valued and understood as individuals.
2. **Communicate Proactively:** Don't just wait for customers to reach out. Proactively share helpful information, tips, updates and exclusive offers tailored to their interests. Set reminders to follow up and check in regularly. This proactive communication strengthens relationships.
3. **Active Listening:** Don't just broadcast messages; actively listen to your customers. This means responding to feedback (positive and negative), conducting surveys, and engaging in conversations on social media. Pay attention to what your customers are saying, not just what you want them to hear.
4. **Open Communication Channels:** Provide multiple avenues for cus-

tomers to reach you – through social media, email, phone support, or even live chat. Make it easy for them to connect with you and have their voices heard.

5. **Provide Excellent Service:** Delivering consistently friendly, knowledgeable and responsive service is crucial. Make sure every customer interaction is a positive experience by training employees well. Quickly resolve any issues or complaints. Going above and beyond with small Service gestures creates powerful goodwill.
6. **Be Genuinely Helpful:** Look for opportunities to provide customers with assistance and value beyond just making a sale. Share expert advice, resources and suggestions tailored to their specific needs and challenges. Position your brand as a trusted partner invested in its success.
7. **Create Experiences:** Strengthen bonds through creating shared experiences that allow customers to interact with and become part of your brand's story. This could include events, contests, exclusive beta programs, co-creation opportunities and more.
8. **Remember Important Details:** Make a note of important details like birthdays, anniversaries, major life events etc. Then reach out with a personalized message, offer or small gift on those occasions. This shows you see them as an individual, not just a customer number.
9. **Implement a Loyalty Program:** A well-designed loyalty or rewards program incentivizes customers to keep engaging with your brand over time. Surprise and delight with unexpected perks and early access to make them feel valued.
10. **Be Responsive on Social Media:** Social media is a hotline for relationship communication. Be present by monitoring, quickly responding to comments/questions, and joining conversations. Invite feedback and implement suggestions to show you're listening.
11. **Get Personal Face-Time:** While digital is convenient, making time for personal face-to-face interactions at events or in-store can really strengthen the human connection. These personal touches provide differentiated experiences customers appreciate.
12. **Partner with Customers:** Look for ways to collaborate with customers,

like co-creation opportunities for product/service feedback or letting them be brand ambassadors. Making customers partners in your journey gives them an emotional investment.

13. **Tell Your Brand Story:** Develop a clear, compelling brand story that resonates emotionally - your founding, values, and differentiators. Share it through diverse content like videos or employee meet-and-greets. Relatable storytelling humanizes the brand.
14. **Build Community:** Foster a sense of community around your product or service where customers can connect with each other and your brand. Facilitate conversation through forums, meetups, social media groups and more. This tribal feeling of belonging is powerful.
15. **Leverage Smart Technology:** Use technologies like CRM databases, automated email campaigns, social media listening and website analytics to help you better understand customers' needs and preferences for more personalized nurturing.
16. **Show Appreciation:** Simple gestures like thanking customers, celebrating milestones or anniversaries with them, and showing gratitude through loyalty programs or surprise benefits can strengthen affinity.
17. **Be Authentic and Transparent:** Customers crave brands they can trust and relate to on a human level. Be genuine in your voice, values and storytelling. Admit mistakes, incorporate feedback and give a peek behind the curtain at times.
18. **Stay Consistent and Reliable:** Consistency in your branding, messaging, quality standards, and overall experience is key. Customers want to know what to expect from your brand at every touchpoint. Familiarity and reliability breed trust over time.

The key is treating customers not just as revenue sources but as individual people to build long-term relationships with through personal connections, superior service and memorable positive experiences. Strong customer relationships breed loyalty, advocacy and lasting brand equity.

Zappos

Zappos is well-known for its exceptional customer service and relationship-building strategies that create raving fans. Some of the key ways they foster customer bonds include:

Personal and Memorable Service: Zappos empowers its customer loyalty team to go above and beyond on each interaction. This includes sending handwritten notes, celebrating customer milestones like birthdays or anniversaries, and taking the extra step to personally research solutions.

In 2011, a Zappos customer service rep named Christen Shepherd received a call from a woman who was going through an incredibly difficult time. The woman shared that her fiancé had recently passed away after a tragic incident, and she had some shoes she needed to return - shoes her late fiancé had actually purchased for her to wear at their upcoming wedding.

Shepherd could have simply processed the return transactionally, but she sensed the emotional weight this return carried for the grieving woman. So instead, she led with empathy and compassion. Shepherd patiently listened as the woman relayed stories and memories about her fiancé on that call, letting her process her grief.

At one point, the woman apologized for taking up so much of Shepherd's time. But Shepherd reassured her that she had nowhere else to be - Zappos encourages reps to stay on calls as long as needed to provide emotional support.

After that initial long call, Shepherd kept checking in with the woman periodically over the next several months as she grieved, offering an understanding ear and helpful resources like counseling recommendations.

Ultimately, the woman expressed feeling so moved by Shepherd's empathy and consistent care during that unimaginably painful period. What could have been an impersonal transaction became a source of healing and relationship-building between the customer and the brand.

In another instance, Zappos customer loyalty team member Shawn was assisting a customer named Robert, who was in a frantic situation. Robert's wedding was just a couple of days away, and he had been unable to find the particular style and colour of shoes he needed for his groomsmen's party.

Robert had struck out locally and was running out of time to get the shoes shipped before the wedding. In a last-ditch effort, he called Zappos late one evening to explain his predicament and ask if they possibly had the shoes in stock.

Unfortunately, Shawn checked, and the shoes Robert needed were not available in Zappos' inventory. At this point, many customer service reps may have simply expressed apologies and ended the call. But Shawn's dedication to helping customers went far beyond.

Shawn recognized the urgency of Robert's situation. So he took it upon himself to search for other online retailers that might have the shoes in stock. After some digging, he found the exact style on a competitor's website that could get the shipment delivered before Robert's wedding.

Rather than simply providing those details to Robert, Shawn took the extra step to place and process the order himself on the other site using Robert's payment information. He ensured the rush shipping and handling were properly applied.

Shawn then followed up with Robert to confirm the order details and delivery timeline, putting his mind at ease that his groomsmen would have their shoes in time for his big day.

Robert was stunned and overwhelmingly grateful that Shawn put in such tremendous effort outside of Zappos' domain, doing whatever it took to solve his problem and personal crisis. For Shawn, it was simply delivering the very best in service, even if it meant engaging with a competitor.

This powerful story, which Zappos has highlighted, exemplifies their commitment to going above and beyond, making personal connections, and unparalleled dedication to customers. It showcases that Zappos reps don't just "close tickets" - they develop relationships and take emotional ownership over customer needs.

Creating Sharable Experiences: Zappos doesn't just sell shoes - it aims to create sharable, buzzworthy experiences for customers. Examples include surprise upgrades to overnight shipping, appearances from the Zappos monkey mascot for kids, and deliveries that sometimes arrive in whimsically decorative boxes.

This element of pleasant surprise and delight gives customers something positive to share with friends and family, turning them into brand evangelists.

Active Listening and Dialogue: Zappos constantly solicits feedback through surveys and encourages open dialogue across its social media channels. This two-way conversation helps Zappos better understand evolving customer needs and continually improve experiences based on that ongoing feedback loop.

One initiative born from this dialogue was the launch of a separate phone line for customers to call and discuss anything—their purchases, sure, but also their lives, their days, or just to chat.

Community Building: Zappos has fostered an incredibly loyal community of brand ambassadors called the Zappos Insights group. These specially-selected members get early product releases, and their unvarnished feedback directly shapes new products and policies.

Members feel valued being part of an exclusive inner circle, while Zappos benefits from their passionate customer perspectives.

Overall, Zappos exemplifies using multi-faceted relationship building, personalized attention and generating sharable positive experiences to cultivate deep emotional connections with customers as valued individuals - not just transactions. This human-centric approach produces legendary customer loyalty and brand evangelism.

Trader Joe's

The grocery chain Trader Joe's has cultivated almost a cult-like following among its customer base by fostering a distinctive brand personality and community experience. Some of the key ways they build relationships include:

Creating a Neighborhood Grocer Feel: Despite being a national chain, Trader Joe's works hard to provide a localized, friendly neighbourhood grocer vibe in each store. Employees are trained to engage customers with genuine conversations, offer samplings, and provide an air of warmth akin to a mom-and-pop shop. This approachable, welcoming atmosphere helps customers feel an emotional connection to their local Trader Joe's.

Fostering Product Enthusiasm: Trader Joe's generates excitement around their private label products by encouraging two-way dialogue with customers. In-store product scouts actively seek out customer feedback and recommendations for potential new items. This gives customers a sense of ownership and personal investment in the brand's offerings.

Surprise and Delight: Trader Joe's is known for frequently rotating unique, seasonal, and quirky item offerings. This element of the unexpected delights customers and keeps them eagerly coming back to explore what's new. Limited-time "cult favourite" products generate major buzz and emotional attachment.

Embracing Transparency: Trader Joe's cultivates trust and authenticity through transparency around their sourcing, ingredients, and environmental practices. Their minimalistic private label packaging highlights this commitment. Customers feel an emotional connection to a brand they perceive as being honest and ethical.

Trader Joe's capitalizes on relatively simple strategies like engaging staff, prompting customer dialogue, delighting with fun surprises, and ethical transparency. But the cumulative effect is that Trader Joe's feels like a neighborhood spot filled with familiar faces and personal investment versus a sterile corporate grocery chain. Customers develop a strong loyalty to that unique experience and a sense of relationship with the brand.

Starbucks

Starbucks is a master at making customers feel like much more than just transactional buyers of coffee. Through deliberate relationship-building strategies, they've turned their brand into a lifestyle experience that fosters fierce loyalty. Some key ways they do this:

The Third Place Experience: Starbucks wants customers to view their stores as an inviting "third place" between home and work. From the cozy club chairs and fireplaces to the free wifi and ambient music, the entire environment is designed to encourage lingering and human connection over coffee.

Customer-Barista Rapport: A key component is building personal relationships between customers and baristas. Baristas make an effort to learn regulars' names and drink orders to provide a "personal touch." This individual recognition makes customers feel valued and part of a privileged inner circle at their local store.

The Starbucks App: Their mobile app allows customers to pay, tip, collect rewards, and receive personalized drink recommendations and special offers. Customized to their preferences, it feels like Starbucks is serving them as an individual, not a number.

Starbucks Rewards: The rewards program captures data to customize offers and further engages customers through gamification and incentives. Members feel like part of an exclusive club getting elite Starbucks experiences.

Community Involvement: Starbucks encourages customers to view stores as neighbourhood "third places" by hosting open mic nights, book clubs, community meetings and more. They position the brand as an integral part of people's local communities and lives.

Transparency: Transparency and authenticity are also key pillars of Starbucks' relationship-building strategy. The brand maintains transparency about its sourcing practices and commitment to ethical sourcing, resonating with customers who value corporate responsibility and sustainability.

Upholders of Values: By taking public stances on social issues that resonate with their customer base's beliefs around sustainability, opportunity, etc.

Starbucks allows customers to feel that their patronage supports a brand that shares its values.

Two-way Communication: The coffee giant also prioritizes two-way engagement, actively interacting with customers on social media platforms and responding to their feedback and concerns. By fostering open communication and creating a sense of community online, Starbucks strengthens its relationship with customers and fosters a loyal fan base.

The combination of personalized experiences, consistency, loyalty reinforcement, local community-building and brand values helps customers form deep, emotional relationships with Starbucks that go far beyond just grabbing a cup of coffee. It becomes a vital part of their lifestyles, and they grow deeply attached to it over time.

LEGO

Facilitating Family Bonding LEGO sets are designed to bring families together for quality bonding time over creative projects. The act of building alongside loved ones facilitates shared experiences, memories, and inside jokes - forming emotional ties to the LEGO brand.

LEGO Clubs/Events: LEGO offers clubs like the LEGO VIP program as well as conventions, contests, and events that allow adult fans and families to connect with both the brand and each other over their shared passion. This fosters a strong sense of community relationship.

Two-Way Dialogue: LEGO directly engages customers through channels like LEGO Ideas, where fans can submit set concepts and vote on designs. Customers feel heard and personally invested in the evolution of LEGO's product lines.

User-Generated Content: LEGO curates and promotes photos, videos and stories created by fans across its own marketing channels. This amplifies customers' emotional connections as co-creators and storytellers alongside the brand.

Nostalgia and Tradition: For many adults, LEGO evokes powerful nostalgia for treasured childhood memories of unbridled creativity. Reconnecting with the brand rekindles those warm emotional associations with LEGO as a constant throughout life. Recognizing this, the brand re-released classic sets alongside innovative themes, bridging generations through a shared love of LEGO. This multi-generational appeal wasn't just about demographics; it was about acknowledging the emotional resonance LEGO held for families, transcending age barriers.

Immersive Brand Experiences: LEGO has created immersive brand experiences centres like LEGOLAND theme parks and LEGO House visitor centres. These destinations allow families to get lost in the LEGO universe through rides, exhibits, and massive brick sculptures that spark awe and deepen brand affinity.

Retail Store Experiences: By transforming its retail stores into interactive playgrounds, LEGO created immersive experiences where customers could engage with the brand on a deeper level. Pick-A-Brick walls allowed for personalized creations, building challenges sparked friendly competition, and play areas brought LEGO adventures to life. These in-store experiences weren't just about transactions; they were about creating lasting memories and strengthening the emotional connection between LEGO and the joy of creation.

Customization Opportunities: Initiatives like the LEGO Bricks & Pieces program let customers order precise elements to personalize or recreate sets. This ability to customize products fuels personal investment.

Behind-the-Scenes Connections: Through media like TV shows, exclusive tours, and interviews with LEGO designers, LEGO provides fans with a rare inside look. Customers feel they have special insider access that fortifies the brand relationship.

Partnerships and Co-Branding: LEGO collaborates with beloved brands like Star Wars, Harry Potter, and Nintendo to create highly-anticipated co-branded sets that unite multiple fan communities and deepen attachments.

Philanthropic Affiliation: Programs like the LEGO Replay initiative to recycle and donate used bricks to kids in need allow customers to feel their patronage has a positive social impact.

In essence, LEGO immerses customers in a relationship that goes beyond just purchasing toys.

Airbnb

Airbnb has revolutionized the travel industry by prioritizing customer relationships and fostering emotional connections within its community. Through personalized experiences, community engagement, and shared values, Airbnb creates a sense of belonging and authenticity that sets it apart from traditional accommodations.

One of Airbnb's key strategies is personalized experiences. Hosts have the freedom to customize their listings, offering unique accommodations and activities tailored to guests' preferences. This personal touch creates a genuine connection between hosts and guests, fostering trust and loyalty.

Community engagement is another cornerstone of Airbnb's approach. The platform encourages open communication through features like host profiles, guest reviews, and messaging platforms. This enables hosts and guests to interact, share recommendations, and build relationships beyond the transaction.

Airbnb also facilitates connections between hosts and guests, often resulting in meaningful relationships. Hosts become ambassadors for their cities, sharing local insights and recommendations, while guests gain a deeper appreciation for the destination through authentic experiences.

Central to Airbnb's success is its promotion of shared values such as inclusivity, diversity, and belonging. By aligning with these values, Airbnb creates an emotional connection with its community, fostering a sense of belonging and acceptance.

Additionally, Airbnb provides robust support and assistance to hosts and guests, ensuring a positive experience for everyone involved. This dedication to customer service strengthens relationships and builds trust in the Airbnb brand.

Moreover, Airbnb recognizes and celebrates the contributions of its hosts through various recognition programs and incentives. This appreciation reinforces the sense of belonging and encourages hosts to continue providing exceptional experiences.

Through loyalty programs, social impact initiatives, user feedback integration, community events, transparent communication, and empowerment through technology, Airbnb demonstrates its commitment to building lasting relationships with its customers.

In conclusion, building relationships with customers is the cornerstone of creating an emotional brand. By prioritizing authenticity, empathy, and consistent communication, brands can foster trust, loyalty, and deep emotional connections with their audience. These connections not only drive customer satisfaction and advocacy but also differentiate the brand in a competitive market, ultimately leading to long-term success and sustainability.

* * *

12

Building A Community of Shared Interests

Samantha tightened her laces and stepped onto the treadmill, firing up the Peloton app on her tablet. As the leaderboard populated with thousands of other members logging in for this live 20-minute HIIT run, she felt a surge of adrenaline. While the voice of her favourite NYC-based instructor, Selena, blasted through her earbuds, Samantha's eyes danced across the screen - giving shout-outs, celebrating milestone achievements, and friendly competitive banter filling the feed.

For Samantha, this was about so much more than just exercising at home. It was plugging into an entire community, a tribe united by their shared passion for levelling up their fitness alongside Peloton's magnetic instructors. No matter her location, she always had this global family to train alongside.

After the pulse-pounding workout, Samantha lingered to chat and swap high-fives with her regular "Riding buddies" like Michael from Perth and Dani in Miami - people who had become Facebook friends and texting pals despite being spread across different continents. They'd get together on the Peloton app to celebrate one another's personal records and breakthroughs or just laugh off a tough day over shared playlists.

This was the beating heart of the Peloton experience—an energetic, supportive community that transcended just following along with videos. Through thoughtfully designed features fostering interaction and engagement, Peloton built a buzzing hive of motivation, accountability, and interpersonal connections.

As Samantha browsed the upcoming schedule of live-ride DJs, artist series, and virtual vacations, she felt a contagious thrill. She wasn't just buying exercise equipment - she was staking her place in a global movement of channeling the power of shared interests into tangible life transformations. And that sense of belonging fueled Samantha to dig deeper into her Peloton practice each day.

Whether indoor cycling, marathon training, learning a new instrument or anything that ignites passion and commitment, humans crave the existential energy that comes from journeying towards meaningful goals alongside others on that same path.

For companies like Peloton, facilitating a community built around shared interests and ambitions is more than just a smart business strategy—it's the key to unlocking powerful emotional connections with their brand.

At its core, the human need for belonging runs deep. We are programmed to seek out tribes we can identify with, find affirmation in, and draw motivation from as we collectively strive towards common objectives. Peloton recognized this fundamental desire and made being part of an inspiring, supportive community a central pillar of their offering.

By designing an immersive social experience into their platform, Peloton allowed members like Samantha to join a worldwide movement unified by their passions for fitness and self-improvement. With just a few taps, she could seamlessly interact with peers, give and receive encouragement, and celebrate shared wins, both big and small.

This facilitated human connection enriched the entire Peloton journey. No longer were members just following impersonal workout videos in isolation. Now, they had an energizing, palpable sense of being part of something larger - a motivated tribe all investing hard work towards collective growth alongside Peloton's magnetic instructors cheering them on.

It was this tribalism, this community built on mutual understanding and shared hopes, that bred the kind of emotional investment Peloton members have in the brand. When people's personal development and identity become intertwined with being part of a supportive collective facilitated by a brand, they aren't simply customers anymore—they're loyalists.

Peloton became more than just exercise equipment; it nurtured the belonging between members around their common interests. People emotionally bonded to the platform as the connective tissue bringing their tribe together to inspire one another. That's the powerful upside brands unlock when strategically building communities - they weave themselves into the very fabric of people's lives, experiences and self-actualization.

The Other Benefits:

- **Brand Advocacy Through Community:** A vibrant community can serve as a powerful marketing tool. Enthusiastic members who are passionate about your brand will naturally share their positive experiences with others, acting as brand advocates. Their genuine endorsements and word-of-mouth recommendations carry significant weight and can help attract new customers to your brand.
- **Valuable Customer Insights:** Communities provide a platform for open communication and feedback. By actively listening to your community members, you gain valuable insights into their needs, preferences, and pain points. This feedback loop allows you to better understand your customers and tailor your products, services, and messaging to meet their expectations effectively.
- **Co-Creation and Innovation:** Engaging your community in co-creation and innovation processes can lead to groundbreaking ideas and solutions. By involving members in product development, content creation, or brainstorming sessions, you tap into a collective pool of creativity, knowledge, and expertise. This collaborative approach not only fosters a sense of ownership among community members but also drives innovation and differentiation for your brand.

Here are some strategies to consider when building a community around shared interests:

- **Identify Your Tribe:** Who are your ideal customers? What are their passions? Once you understand their interests, you can create a community space that caters to them.
- **Foster Common Goals:** Identify the shared interests, passions or objectives that unite your customer base and create experiences that allow them to collectively work towards those common goals as a community. Examples could include fitness challenges, learning courses, customer success groups, etc.
- **Choose the Right Platform:** Establish a platform where like-minded individuals can come together to connect, share, and engage around their shared interests. Online forums, social media groups, or even in-person events can be great platforms for fostering a community. Choose the platform that best suits your target audience and the type of interaction you want to encourage.
- **Provide Value Beyond the Product:** Share tips, advice, content and useful resources related to your industry/customer interests that extend value beyond your core product or service.
- **Facilitate Interaction:** Encourage interaction and collaboration within the community by providing opportunities for members to share their experiences, knowledge, and perspectives. This could include hosting events, organizing discussions or workshops, or facilitating online conversations and content sharing.
- **Foster a Sense of Belonging:** Cultivate a welcoming and inclusive environment where all members feel valued, respected, and supported. Celebrate diversity and encourage members to express themselves authentically without fear of judgment or discrimination.
- **Foster Relationships:** Encourage members to form meaningful connections and relationships with one another based on their shared interests and experiences. Facilitate networking, collaboration, and mentorship opportunities that allow members to support and learn from each other.
- **Highlight Customer Stories:** Regularly spotlight and celebrate specific customers' journeys, achievements, and stories related to your product/service. This reinforces that you value the community as inspirational

individuals, not just buyers.
- **Offer Exclusive Access:** Provide your engaged community with special insider access, sneak peeks, exclusives and advantages that make them feel like privileged members of an inner circle. This breeds deeper affinity.
- **Embrace User-Generated Content:** Curate, promote and weave user-generated content like reviews, photos/videos, interviews and more into your own brand channels and marketing. This amplifies community voices and ownership.
- **Develop Traditions and Rituals:** Create unique traditions, competitions, recurring events or community-building rituals to participate in that become anticipated parts of your shared culture and identity.
- **Foster Sub-Communities:** In addition to the overall unified community, enable smaller niche sub-groups to foster even tighter bonds around specific interests, locations, goals, etc.
- **Co-Creation and Collaboration:** Invite community members to actively participate in developing new products, providing feedback, and collaborating with your brand. This cultivates emotional investment when customers feel their input directly shapes the brand's direction.
- **Influencer and Ambassador Programs:** Identify highly engaged super-fans and community members and empower them as brand ambassadors or influencers. Provide insider access and have them evangelize the message/products authentically to their peers.
- **Gamification and Incentives:** Integrate gamification elements like points, badges, leaderboards and reward/loyalty programs. This engages community members through fun competition and incentivized participation.
- **Behind-the-Scenes Access:** Build connections by giving community members a peek behind-the-curtain at your brand's processes, team members, factories, etc. The insider perspective breeds affinity.
- **Support Meaningful Causes:** If your community members unite around certain values or causes, support relevant philanthropic or social impact initiatives that allow customers to make a difference alongside your brand.

- **Facilitate Mentorship:** Enable experienced community members to mentor new members, sharing expertise and advice. This reinforces the supportive, inclusive bonds within the community.
- **Crowd-Sourced Innovation:** Pose questions, challenges or contests where community members can submit ideas to collectively solve problems, innovate new concepts, name products, etc. Empowering this level of collaboration deepens loyalty.
- **Be Authentic:** Show your brand's personality and connect with your community on a human level.
- **Listen and Adapt:** Continuously listen to the needs, feedback, and preferences of the community members and be willing to adapt and evolve based on their input. This demonstrates a commitment to meeting their needs and ensures that the community remains relevant and valuable over time.
- **Celebrate Successes:** Recognize and celebrate the achievements, milestones, and contributions of community members. This fosters a sense of pride, camaraderie, and shared identity within the community, strengthening the emotional connection and loyalty to the brand.

The key is making your brand the humble host that unites and energizes a community of passionate individuals, giving them a sense of belonging and shared purpose beyond just transactional relationships. Successful communities breed incredibly loyal emotional bonds.

SoulCycle

From the beginning, SoulCycle set out to be much more than just another fitness studio or spin class. Its founders wanted to tap into the deeply human need for belonging and create a tribal community experience revolving around inspirational indoor cycling workouts.

Curated Shared Experiences: SoulCycle designs every aspect of its studio experiences to facilitate feelings of energized togetherness. From the darkened candlelit rooms to the motivational instructors leading the pack through high-intensity rides to the choreographed upper body series—the stage is set for riders to lose themselves in a communal mind-body journey.

Digital Hub: The SoulCycle mobile app and digital platforms allow community members to easily connect outside the studio. Riders can share, upload performance metrics, stream exclusive content, coordinate meetups, and engage in discussions that keep the motivational energy flowing 24/7.

Insider Culture: SoulCycle has developed its own unique language, instructional cues, and cultural identity that breeds a sense of InsiderStatus for devoted riders. Popular instructors develop personal "tribes" of loyal followers. Apparel collaborations reinforce the tribe's style and swagger.

Live Events: To unite the community in person, SoulCycle regularly hosts immersive live events featuring their top instructors leading massive group rides. Riders from all over travel to pack auditoriums or outdoor spaces, coming together in a transcendent shared interest experience.

Instructor as Influencers: SoulCycle's instructors are treated like rock star influencers, each cultivating their own devoted followings. Instructors connect directly with riders through social media, events, and personal brands aligned with SoulCycle's philosophy. This facilitates powerful instructor-rider rapport and tribalism.

Exclusive Access: SoulCycle offers exclusive apparel/merchandise collaborations, insider content, and premium digital/studio perks that reinforce members' sense of gaining special treatment and insider access within the community.

Meaningful Causes: The brand aligns with causes that resonate with its community's values, like feminism, LGBTQ+ rights, and fundraising efforts. This allows riders to feel their community represents shared ideals.

Customer Co-Creation: Crowdsourced playlists, branded hashtags/mantras coined by riders, and other user-generated content are frequently incorporated, making customers integral co-creators of the SoulCycle ethos.

Sub-Communities: While united globally, smaller local "tribes" develop within each SoulCycle studio location, facilitating tight-knit connections among riders taking the same scheduled classes together weekly.

The overarching principle is that SoulCycle immerses customers in a 360-degree community experience far beyond just attending a fitness class. Every touchpoint reinforces belonging to an inspirational tribe, driving one another toward growth. This multidimensional approach breeds powerful emotional loyalty to the brand.

Harley Davidson

The Harley-Davidson community formed organically over several decades, driven by shared values, experiences, and a passion for motorcycles.

For Harley enthusiasts, the brand represents far more than just motorcycles—it's an entire lifestyle and identity centred around ideals of freedom, rebellion, and the fraternity of riders. Harley has become the rallying point for this passionate community that's elevated the brand to a full-fledged subculture.

At the core is Harley's Owners Group (H.O.G.), boasting over 1 million members united globally through local chapters, rallies, events, exclusive benefits, and dedicated digital spaces to connect. H.O.G. gives owners an instant tribe and avenue to foster camaraderie the moment they join.

Harley doubles down on building community through its large-scale, immersive experiential events like the annual Sturgis Motorcycle Rally drawing hundreds of thousands and Harley's 115th Anniversary Milwaukee Celebration. These massive gatherings deepen riders' brand affinity as they join the herd.

Intrinsic to Harley's community is the culture of customization, allowing owners to personalize and make their bikes an expression of individuality. Harley nurtures this through dedicated garage resources and curating inspiration from fan customizations.

The brand also wields longtime riders as influential ambassadors, leveraging their authentic voices to generate excitement, serve as mentors, and reinforce Harley's ideals and lifestyle throughout the community.

Giving back is also intertwined with the Harley owner ethos, as evidenced by philanthropic events like riding rallies and raising millions for veterans' charities each year. This aligns owners' passions with meaningful causes.

Underpinning it all is Harley-Davidson's rich heritage, dating back over a century to its earliest motorcycle origins in the rebel culture of 20th century America. This storied legacy is something modern riders resonate with and aspire to be part of through ownership.

Harley has capitalized expertly, making shared experiences and camaraderie cornerstones. Owning and riding a Harley motorcycle transcends transportation—it's about fully embracing the freedom, thrills, scenery, and unforgettable adventures of the open-road lifestyle. Riders form profound bonds through these mutual adrenaline-laced memories.

By honouring its roots, building personal connections, enabling owners' self-expression through customization and making the Harley lifestyle a philosophy of liberty and shared ideals, the brand has created a fervent global community profoundly invested in its identity and values. This 360-degree cultivation of personal identity and meaning is what elevates the relationship between Harley and its riders to such an emotionally charged, tribalistic level.

Sephora's "Beauty Insider" Community

While Sephora is a leading beauty retailer, the brand has cultivated a powerful community philosophy that allows customers to become "insiders" who feel a sense of belonging to something bigger.

Beauty Insider Loyalty Program: The Beauty Insider program provides the gateway, rewarding customers with points, customized product recommendations, birthday gifts and exclusive access to events/launches. This incentivizes consistent engagement.

Social Media Communities: Sephora maintains extremely active, devoted communities across platforms like Facebook, Instagram, Twitter and even Reddit. These allow customers to discuss products, share looks, and inspire one another.

In-Store Beauty Services: Sephora's retail locations offer complimentary in-person beauty services like mini-facials and makeovers. These services facilitate personal connections between customers and Sephora experts.

Sephora Squads: These are private social groups created by customers on Facebook around shared interests, locations or affiliations. Sephora provides resources for these ultra-passionate niche communities.

Beauty Insider Community Weeks: Sephora hosts these week-long virtual and in-person events featuring masterclasses from brand founders, meet-and-greets with influencers, and massive community contests/giveaways.

Skill-Sharing: The brand provides platforms for customers to share makeup artistry skills through how-to content, enabling peer-to-peer education within the community.

User Ratings/Reviews: Customers' honest ratings and reviews are prominently featured, making the shopping experience a community-guided one based on peer advice and feedback.

In-App Virtual Services: Through capabilities like Virtual Artist lip-try-ons, Sephora creates personalized, guided digital experiences that connect customers to experts and to each other.

Community Influence: The Community Admired program empowers top customers to preview and influence future Sephora products/merchandising through direct feedback loops.

Brand Collaborations: Co-created product lines with community-beloved influencers and brands allow the Sephora community to feel their voices and preferences directly shape offerings.

By making community-building and customer connectedness priorities across all its consumer touchpoints, Sephora cultivates incredibly high engagement and emotional investment from its members, who see it as much more than just another beauty brand.

In conclusion, building a community of shared interests is not just about bringing people together; it's about fostering deep emotional connections that transcend transactional relationships. By creating inclusive, engaging spaces where members can connect, collaborate, and celebrate shared passions, brands can cultivate loyalty, advocacy, and long-term success.

The strategies outlined provide a roadmap for brands to nurture meaningful communities that serve as powerful catalysts for brand growth, innovation, and enduring emotional bonds with their audience.

* * *

13

Sell Identity

Nadia studied her reflection one last time before leaving her room. Her emerald green Dynalo cycling jersey with its distinctive geometric pattern stood out vividly against her toned physique. But this meticulously designed athletic apparel represented so much more than just performance wear.

As she pedalled through the city streets towards her favourite coffee shop meetup, Nadia noticed the occasional head turn and nods of recognition from passing cyclists. They immediately identified her as a fellow member of the Dynalo tribe - cyclists forging their own path at the intersection of style, endurance and nonconformity.

The Dynalo jersey attracted like-minded spirits craving superior technical fabrics but also a uniform broadcasting their *identity as movers, shakers and urban trailblazers.* At the cafe, Nadia locked up her cycle and strode inside, sleek roadie sunglasses still shielding her eyes.

"Looking fresh, Dee!" The barista grinned, immediately recognizing her regular order. Most coffee shops simply had customers, but for Dynalo riders, this was an integral pit stop in their communal journey.

Shortly after, Nadia's crew gradually filtered in, hailing her with aftershocks and high fives. Each distinct Dynalo kit pattern represented a unique individual's personal flair and personality. Yet together, they formed an unmistakable system by which fellow pathfinders from all walks of life could identify one another's divergent mindsets.

SELL IDENTITY

More than apparel, Dynalo created an entire iconography that translated the pleasures and grit of cycling's soul into a bold, stylish statement. The clothes allowed wearers to advertise their passion, lifestyle and tribal allegiance while propelling themselves in radical ways.

Later, as their group ride kicked off, Nadia felt a sense of energy rippling through the line of kaleidoscopic jerseys. They weren't just athletes but identities in seamless forward motion united in bucking staid sportswear conventions. Every bead of perspiration and every climb conquered became a testament to their Dynalo spirit, building their legend.

At the crest of a ridge offering panoramic views, the group's camaraderie is embodied in their eye-catching uniforms. They celebrated with irreverent hand signals that only their kindred tribe understood. At that moment, Dynalo stood for an entire identity—one of resilience, radical aesthetics, and forging their own paths day by day.

By infusing its highly technical garments with distinct, stylized designs that begged for a second look, Dynalo allowed customers to showcase their identity as boundary-pushers, turn the urban landscape into their own canvas, and forge emotional connections with a brand representing the beauty of unorthodox motion.

Creating products that allow customers to "advertise their identity" and outwardly express who they are is a powerful strategy for building emotional brand connections.

At its core, humans have an innate desire for self-expression and want to surround themselves with brands that give them an avenue to showcase their values, personalities, and lifestyles to the world. We use products as extensions of our identity, signalling our affiliations and aspirations.

Dynalo recognized this by going beyond just manufacturing high-performance cycling apparel. Their distinctive, stylized designs essentially become mobile canvases, allowing riders to paint their personal attitudes and philosophies onto the urban landscape.

By wearing the Dynalo uniform, customers aren't just being consumers - they're advertising their identity as non-conformists, aesthetic connoisseurs, and pioneers charting new paths. The apparel becomes a striking badge of allegiance, allowing them to attract like-minded individuals into their tribe.

The clothes permit wearers to make a statement, challenging others to take a second look and either join the revolution or remain spectators. This identity-driven approach allows Dynalo to forge incredible brand loyalty and affinity, as customers feel the brand fundamentally "gets" them and hands them tools to telegraph who they truly are to the world.

Great brands striving for emotional connections must grasp this—people don't simply buy products; they buy vehicles for identity. By channelling this core truth into offerings that amplify customers' sense of self, brands can cultivate powerful, lasting relationships that paid advertising alone cannot replicate.

How to Sell Identity?

Selling identity as a factor in building emotional branding involves aligning your brand with the values, aspirations, and lifestyles of your target audience. It goes beyond promoting products or services; it's about becoming a symbol of the identity your customers want to embody. Here's how to do it:

Understanding Your Customer's Identity: To effectively sell identity, you need to understand your target audience on a deeper level. This means going beyond demographics and delving into their values, aspirations, and social circles. What story are they telling about themselves, and how does your brand fit into that narrative?

Associating Your Brand with Their Identity: Craft a brand image and messaging that resonates with your customer's desired identity. Whether they're adventurous, eco-conscious, or creative, your brand should embody those values and become a symbol of what they aspire to be. Imbue your products with distinct aesthetics, design languages, and iconic signifiers that become potent symbols representing your customers' identities.

Create emotional connections through storytelling: Use narratives that showcase how your product or service helps customers achieve their goals, express their values, and live the life they dream of. By tapping into their emotions, you can forge a deeper bond with your audience.

Focus on the aspirational, not just the functional aspects of your brand: While functionality is important, emphasize the emotional benefits your product or service offers. How does it make your customers feel about themselves? How does it help them live the life they aspire to?

Offer Customization and Co-Creation: Allow customers to put their personal stamp on products through customization, limited editions, and opportunities to give input that makes them invested co-creators.

Amplify Through Influencers: Identify and equip influential individuals firmly embodying the identities you represent to serve as inspiring beacons, showcasing how your brand allows self-expression.

Consistency and authenticity are key: Maintain consistency and authenticity across all brand touchpoints. Your messaging, actions, and experiences should align seamlessly with the identity you're promoting. Inconsistencies or inauthenticity can erode trust and undermine the emotional connection you're striving to

Moreover, selling an identity entails enabling customers to showcase their identity proudly. Your products or services should be designed in a way that allows customers to outwardly express their identity. In essence, they become ambassadors for your brand, advertising their identity through their association with your offerings.

The core goal is positioning your brand's products as powerful tools and symbols that customers can use to outwardly showcase their personalities, values, tastes, ambitions and affiliations to the world.

Making customers "walking aspirational billboards" for who they truly want to be while providing the community and culture to back it up is what breeds intense emotional brand devotion.

iPod

In the early 2000s, Apple pulled off one of the most brilliant examples of making a product an extension of people's identities with the iconic iPod. From its distinctive design elements to its very business model, the iPod transformed how we expressed ourselves through music in outrageously cool and personal ways.

Perhaps the most subtle yet genius aspect was the iPod's white earbuds. In a sea of black headphones at the time, those unmistakable white cables immediately caught the eye and became a subculture signifier whenever spotted. They advertised, "Hey, I'm an iPod owner", in an instant. Wearing them sent a signal that you were part of Apple's elite cohort of design devotees.

More than utility, music has long been intrinsically tied to personal expression and self-identity. The artists, genres, and sounds we connect with become core tenets of how we outwardly project our moods, interests and personalities to the world. The iPod's game-changing ability to hold thousands of songs made everyone's highly individualized musical identity seamlessly mobile for the first time.

Apple brilliantly capitalized on this with its iconic "Silhouette" ad campaign. The minimalist visuals depicted a user's glowing white silhouette with unmistakable iPod and earbuds, dancing avant-garde against vivid colour backgrounds. These images didn't just tout Product features—they boasted the iPod as THE premiere lifestyle accessory for defining your individuality through music.

While the iPod's physical design was an identity statement in itself, Apple took it a step further by reimagining how we acquired and consumed that personal soundtrack. The iTunes Music Store and seamless iPod/iTunes integration allowed users to extend their identities into a customized music library.

Suddenly, every individual could become their own highly curated DJ, meticulously assembling playlists that captured their current moods, backgrounds, influences and aspirations in a living musical pastiche. What you chose to download onto your iPod became an intimate psychological mirror of your persona at that moment in time.

With those iconic white earbuds in, iPod fans weren't just listening to music—they were immersing themselves in a precise audio identity they'd purposefully crafted to the most granular detail. Every song became an extraordinary public articulation to the world around them.

In cultivating the iPod's flawless integration of hardware, software and limitless music accessibility, Apple singlehandedly turned digital music players into identity accessories. No longer just functional devices, iPods became highly visible emblems of personality, creativity, and membership in a forward-thinking lifestyle tribe that understood the immense power of curation and personal expression through art.

By infusing so much individualism into what was ostensibly just a media player, Apple unknowingly transformed the humble iPod into one of the most powerful modern mobile status symbols of identity ever created. Those white earbuds didn't just beam your music to you—they broadcast precisely who you were to anyone watching, whether they got the message or not.

Lululemon

At first glance, Lululemon appears to simply sell high-end athletic apparel for yoga, running and working out. But look closer, and you'll realize the brand has masterfully positioned itself as an outfitter for an entire lifestyle—an identity transcending just the clothing itself.

The distinctive Lululemon logo and styles have become synonymous with a particular set of ideals and mindsets that its customers buy into. The multipurpose apparel functions as a symbolic uniform, allowing wearers to outwardly express their commitment to living "The Sweatlife."

The Sweatlife identity Lululemon has cultivated goes far beyond just physical exercise. It encapsulates an entire ethical framework and approach to life, prioritizing mindfulness, goal-setting, personal growth, balance and making conscious choices. In many ways, the apparel is simply the outward packaging for this larger inspirational philosophy.

Becoming a Lululemon customer automatically enters a like-minded community of individuals who bond over shared journeys of self-actualization, positivity, and holistic well-being. The brand's clothing serves as an instant symbol, a special suit of armour that reminds wearers of their higher aspirations each time they suit up.

Lululemon stores function as community hubs offering free yoga classes, ambassadors to connect with, and guidance for living The Sweatlife more fully. Employees warmly welcome customers into this tribe, acting as lifestyle outfitters helping them "look the part" through their clothing while embodying the identity.

Beyond just the physical products, Lululemon surrounds customers with messaging and experiences that reinforce the identity's key pillars. Their apps, fitness challenges, ambassador programs, and global retreats all emphasize ideals like entrepreneurship, personal growth, health, and contributing to something greater than oneself.

Ford Mustang and Selling Identity Through Ads

The first Ford Mustang revolutionized automotive marketing by targeting the young and adventurous demographic of the 1960s and crafting ads that tapped into their desires for status, freedom, and personal expression. Understanding that this generation sought excitement and wanted to showcase their individuality, Ford designed the Mustang with sleek lines, powerful engines, and customizable options to appeal to their sense of style and identity.

The iconic ads for the first Mustang models were strategically crafted to help this demographic show off their newfound status and personality. They portrayed the Mustang not just as a car but as a symbol of transformation and empowerment. For example, in the ad featuring Wolfgang(a fictional character), the narrative humorously depicted an ordinary individual becoming a sensation after owning a Mustang, tapping into the desire for fame and admiration among the target audience.

"Wolfgang used to give harpsichord recitals for a few close friends. Then he

bought a Mustang . . . What happened? Sudden fame! Fortune! Adulation of millions! Being a Mustanger brought out the wolf in Wolfgang. What could it do for you?"

Similarly, the ad featuring Desmond(Another fictional character) highlighted the theme of personal empowerment and allure, suggesting that owning a Mustang could elevate one's confidence and attractiveness.

"Desmond was afraid to let the cat out...until he got his Mustang. Mustang! A car that makes weak men strong, strong men invincible. Desmond traded in his Persian kitten for an heiress. He had to. She followed him home. (It's inevitable.... Mustangers have more fun)."

By targeting the aspirations and desires of young consumers, these ads effectively positioned the Mustang as more than just a mode of transportation—it was a lifestyle statement that allowed individuals to express themselves and stand out from the crowd.

Toyota Prius

Toyota Prius Hybrid revolutionized the automotive industry by tapping into the growing desire for eco-friendly products and leveraging identity-based marketing strategies to appeal to consumers' sense of responsibility and social status. Despite facing criticism for its unconventional styling and higher price compared to non-green luxury cars, the Prius became a symbol of environmental consciousness and societal status.

Research has shown that consumers are willing to pay a premium for eco-friendly products, as it allows them to showcase their altruistic nature and demonstrate their commitment to environmental sustainability. In a world where being seen as environmentally conscious is increasingly important, the Prius offered consumers an opportunity to align themselves with these values and broadcast their identity to the world.

The Prius's distinctive design and hybrid-only format reinforced its association with eco-friendliness, making it a clear choice for consumers looking to make a statement about their values. Unlike other hybrid models that blend in with their non-green counterparts, the Prius stood out as a visible symbol of environmental responsibility.

In contrast, brands like Maruti and Honda failed to capitalize on the identity-based marketing opportunity presented by hybrid technology. Models like the Maruti Ciaz and Honda Civic offered hybrid options but lacked clear differentiation from their non-green counterparts, making it difficult for consumers to showcase their altruistic nature through their vehicle choices.

By positioning itself as the ultimate eco-friendly car, the Prius appealed to consumers' desire to be seen as environmentally conscious and socially responsible. In doing so, Toyota not only captured a significant share of the hybrid car market but also solidified the Prius as a cultural icon synonymous with sustainability and social status. Through effective identity-based marketing, the Toyota Prius Hybrid successfully transformed a functional product into a symbol of personal identity and societal values.

In conclusion, selling identity as a factor in emotional branding is about understanding your audience deeply, aligning your brand with their values, and crafting compelling narratives that resonate with their aspirations. It's about creating emotional connections and enabling customers to proudly express their identity through your brand. When executed effectively, this approach fosters strong emotional bonds, driving loyalty and long-term success for your brand.

* * *

14

Customer Empowerment

It was a small artisanal chocolate shop nestled in a charming neighbourhood. The founder, Samantha, had a passion for creating delectable confections that not only tantalized the taste buds but also touched the hearts of her customers.

Samantha understood that building an emotional brand went beyond just offering high-quality chocolates. She wanted her customers to feel a deep connection with her shop, a sense of belonging and emotional resonance.

One day, Samantha had an idea. She decided to invite her customers to share their personal stories and memories associated with chocolate. With each story, she would craft a unique flavour profile, capturing the essence of that particular tale.

Word quickly spread about Samantha's innovative approach, and customers flocked to her shop, eager to share their narratives. A young man recounted how his grandmother's hot chocolate recipe brought warmth and comfort during cold winter nights. Samantha meticulously recreated the blend, infusing it with hints of cinnamon and a touch of vanilla, evoking the nostalgic embrace of a grandmother's love.

Another customer shared the bittersweet memory of a first date gone wrong, yet the evening was salvaged by a shared indulgence in a rich, dark chocolate truffle. Samantha crafted a truffle with a hint of espresso, capturing the complexity of that pivotal moment.

As the stories poured in, Samantha's chocolates became more than just confections; they became tangible representations of the customers' own emotional journeys. Each bite was a gateway to cherished memories, rekindling the feelings and sentiments that made those moments so special.

Customers felt empowered, knowing that their stories had been immortalized in the very chocolates they savored. They developed a profound emotional connection with Samantha's brand, as it had become an extension of their own lives.

Word of mouth spread like wildfire, and Samantha's chocolate shop became a destination for those seeking not just a culinary experience but also a chance to share their stories and have them brought to life through the art of chocolate making.

Through customer empowerment, Samantha successfully built an emotional brand that resonated deeply with her customers. Her shop became a sanctuary where memories were celebrated, emotions were embraced, and the simple act of indulging in chocolate transcended mere indulgence, becoming a deeply personal and meaningful experience.

Customer empowerment is a crucial aspect of building an emotional brand, extending beyond merely delivering good service. It involves granting customers the autonomy and tools to make informed decisions, personalize their experiences, and feel like valued partners in shaping the brand. By empowering customers, brands can achieve several benefits:

Firstly, customer empowerment leads to increased customer satisfaction. When customers feel empowered, they perceive themselves as being in control of their interactions with the brand, resulting in a more positive and fulfilling experience overall.

Secondly, empowering customers fosters enhanced brand loyalty. When customers feel valued and respected by a brand, it strengthens the emotional connection they have with the brand, leading to greater loyalty and advocacy.

Moreover, customer empowerment provides brands with valuable insights into customer needs, preferences, and pain points. By giving customers a voice and involving them in decision-making processes, brands can gain invaluable feedback that informs product development and service improvements.

Lastly, empowered customers are more likely to become brand advocates. When customers feel empowered and satisfied with their experiences, they are more inclined to spread positive word-of-mouth and recommend the brand to others, thereby amplifying the brand's reach and impact.

Strategies for Customer Empowerment:

1. **Personalization:** Empowered customers expect personalized experiences that cater to their unique preferences and needs. Brands can empower customers by offering customization options, personalized recommendations, and tailored communication channels. By allowing customers to shape their interactions with the brand according to their preferences, brands can foster a sense of ownership and connection.

2. **Co-creation:** Customer empowerment involves inviting customers to actively participate in the creation and development of products, services, and brand experiences. Brands can leverage customer feedback, insights, and ideas to co-create offerings that better meet customer needs and preferences. By involving customers in the innovation process, brands demonstrate a commitment to listening and responding to their customers' voices, which strengthens trust and loyalty.

3. **Transparency:** Empowered customers expect transparency from brands regarding their practices, policies, and values. Brands can empower customers by being open and honest about their operations, sourcing, and impact. By providing transparent information, brands empower customers to make informed decisions and align their values with those of the brand. Transparency builds trust and credibility, which are essential for building emotional connections with customers.

4. **Self-service:** Customer empowerment involves providing customers with the tools and resources they need to solve problems and address their needs independently. Brands can empower customers by offering self-service options such as online support portals, knowledge bases,

and community forums. By enabling customers to find answers and solutions on their own terms, brands demonstrate respect for their autonomy and empower them to take control of their experiences.

5. **Advocacy:** Empowered customers are more likely to become brand advocates who actively promote and recommend the brand to others. Brands can empower customers by providing opportunities for them to share their experiences, reviews, and testimonials. By amplifying the voices of satisfied customers, brands harness the power of word-of-mouth marketing and build a community of brand advocates who contribute to the brand's emotional appeal.

6. **Customer Education:** Another important aspect of customer empowerment is education. Brands can empower customers by providing them with relevant information, resources, and guidance to help them make informed decisions. By educating customers about product features, usage tips, industry trends, and best practices, brands empower them to navigate their purchasing journey confidently and effectively. Customer education builds trust and credibility, strengthens relationships, and enhances the overall customer experience.

Overall, customer empowerment is essential for building an emotional brand as it enables customers to engage with the brand on their own terms, fostering a sense of ownership, trust, and loyalty.

Spotify

Spotify isn't just a music streaming platform; it's a powerful tool for self-expression and musical discovery. They've understood the importance of customer empowerment and woven it into the very fabric of their user experience. Here's how Spotify empowers its listeners:

- **The Power of Choice:** Unlike traditional radio, Spotify offers an ocean of music at your fingertips. Users can curate playlists, explore genres, discover new artists – the control lies entirely with them. This empowers listeners to create a sonic identity that reflects their unique tastes and moods.

- **Personalization on Autopilot:** Spotify's algorithms learn from your listening habits and recommend new music based on your preferences. This "Discover Weekly" or "Release Radar" feature empowers listeners to discover new music without the hassle, fostering a sense of serendipitous exploration.
- **Collaboration and Community:** Spotify allows users to follow friends and see their listening activity. Collaborative playlists and social features empower music lovers to connect, share their discoveries, and build a community around shared musical tastes. This fosters a sense of belonging, making the music-listening experience more social and interactive.
- **User-Generated Content:** Spotify empowers its users to create their own podcasts. This allows anyone with a story to share their voice and build a following, further enriching the Spotify experience and empowering creators.
- **Wrapped:** Spotify's annual Wrapped campaign is a masterclass in customer empowerment. Users get personalized insights into their listening habits, showcasing their top artists, genres, and listening minutes. This playful presentation of data empowers listeners to celebrate their unique musical journeys and share them with friends, fostering a sense of community and fun.
- **Empowerment Through Knowledge:** Providing educational resources or tutorials empowers customers to get the most out of your product or service. Spotify achieves this through curated playlists that educate users on specific genres or artists, or even offering playlists designed for specific activities (focus, workout, etc.).
- **Empowerment Through Choice in Consumption:** Spotify offers flexible subscription tiers or pay-as-you-go options. This empowers users to choose a plan that best fits their needs and budget. Spotify offers a free tier with limited features alongside premium tiers with ad-free listening

and higher-quality audio.
- **Empowerment Through Feedback and Co-Creation:** Spotify actively solicits user feedback on new features or upcoming changes. This empowers users to feel like their voice matters and can influence the future of the platform. Spotify uses A/B testing and user feedback to refine its features and personalize the experience based on user preferences.
- **Empowerment Through Recognition and Reward:** Spotify recognizes "Superfans" for artists based on their listening habits, fostering a sense of community and appreciation.
- **Offline Listening:** Spotify Premium subscribers have the option to download songs and playlists for offline listening, allowing them to enjoy their favorite music even without an internet connection. This empowers customers by providing flexibility and convenience, especially in situations where internet access may be limited or unavailable.

By empowering its users to curate their own musical experiences, discover new sounds, and connect with fellow music lovers, Spotify goes beyond just delivering music. They create a platform for self-expression, discovery, and community. This emotional connection fuels brand loyalty and positions Spotify not just as a music streaming service, but as a companion on your unique sonic adventure.

Gopro

Gopro isn't just an action camera company; they're enablers of epic adventures and storytellers. Their focus on customer empowerment goes beyond the technical aspects of their cameras and delves into empowering users to capture and share their passions with the world.

- **Simple and Intuitive Controls:** GoPro cameras are renowned for their user-friendly design. Simple controls and a focus on durability empower even novice users to capture high-quality footage in challenging envi-

ronments. This removes technical barriers and allows users to focus on the adventure itself.
- **Extensive Ecosystem of Mounts and Accessories:** GoPro offers a vast array of mounts and accessories, empowering users to capture their experiences from unique perspectives. Whether it's a helmet mount for a mountain bike ride or a chest mount for surfing, GoPro empowers users to tell their stories from the heart of the action.
- **Quik App for Effortless Editing:** GoPro's Quik app allows users to easily edit their footage on the go. With intuitive editing tools and pre-loaded templates, GoPro empowers users to transform raw footage into captivating stories, even without advanced editing skills. This empowers them to share their adventures quickly and seamlessly.
- **User-Generated Content Platform: GoPro Channel:** The GoPro Channel is a platform brimming with user-generated content. GoPro empowers users to share their adventures with a global audience, inspiring others and fostering a sense of community. This platform celebrates user creativity and positions GoPro as more than a camera company; it's a community of passionate adventurers.
- **Challenges and Awards:** GoPro regularly hosts user-generated content challenges with exciting prizes. This empowers users to push their creative boundaries and showcase their talents. It fosters a sense of friendly competition and recognition within the GoPro community.
- **Educational Resources and Tutorials:** GoPro offers a wealth of educational resources and tutorials online. These include tips on capturing specific types of footage, mastering camera settings for different activities, and even post-production editing techniques. Empowering users with knowledge allows them to get the most out of their GoPro cameras and capture stunning visuals, fostering a sense of accomplishment and creative exploration.
- **Community Building Through Social Media:** GoPro has a strong presence on social media platforms like Instagram and YouTube. They actively engage with their audience, respond to comments and questions, and highlight user-generated content. This fosters a sense of community and

belonging, making GoPro users feel like part of something bigger than just owning a camera.
- **Ambassador Programs:** GoPro has a network of GoPro athletes and ambassadors who are passionate adventurers and skilled storytellers. These ambassadors inspire others through their adventures and showcase the capabilities of GoPro cameras. This empowerment extends beyond everyday users, fostering a sense of aspiration and motivating users to push their own creative boundaries.
- **Openness to Feedback and Collaboration:** GoPro actively solicits feedback from its user base. They use online forums, social media channels, and customer surveys to gather insights on product development and feature improvements. This empowers users to feel like their voices are heard and valued, fostering a sense of co-creation and collaboration.

Through these strategies, GoPro goes beyond simply selling action cameras. They empower their customers to become skilled storytellers, valued members of a community, and active participants in shaping the future of the brand. This holistic approach to customer empowerment fosters a strong emotional connection that fuels brand loyalty and positions GoPro as a brand synonymous with adventure and creative self-expression.

Amazon Prime

Amazon Prime isn't just a fast-shipping membership; it's a package of benefits designed to empower customers and elevate their shopping experience. Here's how Amazon Prime fosters customer empowerment:

a. Convenience at Your Fingertips:

- **Free, Fast Shipping:** Prime membership eliminates the wait and empowers customers to plan their purchases around their needs, not shipping timelines. This convenience allows them to control when they receive

their items, reducing stress and frustration.
- **Unlimited Streaming Options:** Prime Video offers a vast library of movies and TV shows, empowering users to choose what they want to watch whenever they want. This control over entertainment eliminates reliance on traditional cable packages and empowers users to curate their own viewing experience.
- **Early Access to Deals:** Prime members receive exclusive access to Lightning Deals and other sales before the general public. This empowers them to snag the best deals and feel like they're getting an advantage, fostering a sense of satisfaction and control over their shopping experience.

b. **Empowerment Through Choice and Control:**

- **Multiple Membership Tiers:** Amazon offers different Prime membership tiers, allowing customers to choose the plan that best suits their needs and budget. This empowers them to control their spending and get the most value out of their membership.
- **Try Before You Buy:** Prime Wardrobe allows members to try on clothes at home before committing to a purchase. This empowers them to shop with confidence and avoid the hassle of returns for ill-fitting items. This level of control fosters a sense of security and reduces shopping anxiety.
- **Manage Subscriptions with Ease:** Prime members can easily manage their subscriptions to various services like music streaming or cloud storage. This empowers them to control their recurring expenses and tailor their Prime experience to their evolving needs.

c. **Building Trust and Transparency:**

- **Free Trials and Money-Back Guarantees:** Amazon offers generous free trials for Prime memberships. This empowers customers to try the service before committing, fostering trust and reducing the risk associated with signing up. Additionally, Amazon's transparent return policy allows for easy returns if customers are unsatisfied, further empowering them to

control their shopping experience.
- **24/7 Customer Support:** Prime members have access to dedicated customer support around the clock. This empowers them to get help and resolve issues quickly and efficiently, fostering a sense of security and valued membership.

d. **Empowerment Through Knowledge and Education:**

- **Product Reviews and Ratings:** Amazon prioritizes customer reviews and ratings, empowering users to make informed purchasing decisions. This access to real user experiences empowers customers to feel like active participants in the shopping process, not just passive consumers.
- **Buying Guides and Educational Content:** Amazon offers comprehensive buying guides and educational content for various product categories. This empowers customers to research products, compare features, and make confident purchasing decisions without relying solely on marketing claims.

e. **Empowering Customers as Part of a Community:**

- **Amazon Vine Program:** The Amazon Vine program empowers reviewers with early access to new products in exchange for honest reviews. This fosters a sense of community and recognition for valuable customer contributions, further enriching everyone's shopping experience.
- **Amazon Forums and Social Media:** Amazon forums and social media communities allow Prime members to connect with each other, share shopping tips, and get product recommendations. This empowers customers to learn from each other and fosters a sense of belonging to a community of savvy shoppers.

Amazon Prime is not just about fast shipping and exclusive deals; it's about giving customers the knowledge, control, and resources to make informed decisions throughout their shopping journey. This empowerment fosters trust, builds a sense of community, and positions Prime membership as a valuable tool for smart and informed shoppers.

In conclusion, customer empowerment plays a pivotal role in emotional brand building by enhancing satisfaction, fostering loyalty, providing valuable insights, and cultivating advocacy. By offering personalization, co-creation opportunities, transparency, self-service options, advocacy platforms, and educational resources, brands empower customers to engage authentically and build meaningful connections.

* * *

15

Emotional Appeal in Advertisements

Nadiya was a young filmmaker with a gift for capturing the human experience in raw and authentic glory. While her peers were fixated on the latest special effects or blockbuster formulas, Nadiya's true passion lay in telling stories that resonated with the deepest recesses of the human soul.

One day, Nadiya was approached by a beverage company that had struggled to connect with consumers on an emotional level. Their products were high-quality, but their marketing campaigns had failed to create a lasting impression. It was then that Nadiya saw an opportunity to showcase the power of emotional appeal.

Instead of crafting a conventional advertisement, Nadiya embarked on a journey to capture the essence of human connections and the profound role that shared moments play in our lives. She travelled to remote corners of the world, immersing herself in diverse cultures and communities, observing the universal language of human emotion that transcended borders and boundaries.

In a small village in rural Asia, Nadiya witnessed a family gathering for a traditional ceremony, where generations came together to celebrate their bonds over a simple cup of tea. The warmth, the laughter, and the sense of belonging were palpable, reminding her that even the most ordinary moments could hold extraordinary significance.

Halfway across the globe, she found herself in a bustling city where a group of friends huddled around a street vendor's cart, sipping steaming cups of coffee as they shared stories, dreams, and the occasional inside joke. It was a reminder that even in the midst of chaos, human connections could create oases of comfort and camaraderie.

With each encounter, Nadiya wove together a tapestry of human experiences, capturing the essence of how simple beverages could serve as catalysts for forging bonds, creating memories, and celebrating the richness of life's shared moments.

The resulting film was a masterpiece, devoid of overt product placement or sales pitches. Instead, it was a poetic exploration of the universal human need for connection, told through the lens of shared cups and the stories they contained.

When the film was unveiled, it struck a profound chord with audiences worldwide. People saw themselves reflected in the authentic moments captured on screen, reminding them of the profound impact that simple gestures and shared experiences could have on their lives.

The beverage company's brand was forever transformed, no longer just a purveyor of products but a facilitator of human connections and a symbol of the moments that truly mattered. Nadiya's masterful use of emotional appeal turned a simple marketing campaign into a profound celebration of the human experience, forging an indelible emotional bond between the brand and its customers.

The Emotional Appeal

Emotional appeal in advertisements is a crucial factor in building an emotional brand. It's one of the most powerful tools brands have to connect with consumers on a deeper level and create a lasting impression.

Importance of Emotional Appeal:

- **Bypasses Logic and Goes Straight to the Heart:** Facts and figures can be persuasive, but emotional appeals tap into our desires, fears, hopes, and

dreams. This creates a stronger connection than simply listing product features.
- **Memorable and Shareable:** Ads that evoke emotions are more likely to be remembered and shared with others. This organic word-of-mouth marketing strengthens the brand's emotional connection with a wider audience.
- **Builds Brand Loyalty:** When consumers connect with a brand on an emotional level, they're more likely to become loyal customers and advocates for the brand.
- **Differentiating from Competitors:** In today's competitive marketplace, emotional appeal in advertisements helps brands stand out and differentiate themselves from competitors. Brands that successfully evoke emotions and create authentic connections with consumers can carve out a unique position in the market, fostering brand preference and loyalty.
- **Humanizing the Brand:** Emotional advertisements help humanize brands by showcasing their values, personality, and empathy. When brands convey emotions authentically, they become more relatable and trustworthy in the eyes of consumers.

The Emotional Toolkit: Different Emotional Appeals

In advertising and branding, various emotional appeals are employed to evoke specific responses and achieve desired effects. Here are some of the different appeals commonly used:

1. **Happiness and Joy:** Appeals that evoke feelings of happiness, joy, and positivity are often used to create a sense of optimism and well-being associated with the brand. These advertisements aim to uplift the audience's mood and leave them with a positive impression of the brand.
2. **Nostalgia:** Nostalgic appeals tap into fond memories of the past, evoking feelings of sentimentality and longing. Brands often use nostalgic

imagery or references to connect with consumers on an emotional level, leveraging the power of shared experiences and cultural references.
3. **Fear and Anxiety**: Advertisements that elicit feelings of fear or anxiety aim to highlight potential risks or problems that the audience may face. By creating a sense of urgency or concern, these appeals motivate consumers to take action to avoid negative outcomes or consequences.
4. **Empathy and Compassion**: Appeals that evoke empathy and compassion appeal to consumers' emotions by highlighting the struggles or challenges faced by others. Brands may use storytelling or real-life scenarios to connect with consumers on a human level, fostering a sense of understanding and solidarity.
5. **Aspiration and Inspiration:** Appeals centred around aspiration and inspiration tap into consumers' desires for self-improvement, success, or fulfilment. These advertisements often showcase idealized lifestyles, achievements, or experiences that consumers aspire to, motivating them to pursue their goals with the help of the brand.
6. **Surprise and Intrigue**: Appeals that surprise or intrigue the audience aim to capture their attention and curiosity. By presenting unexpected or unconventional content, these advertisements stand out from the crowd and leave a memorable impression on viewers.
7. **Humour and Entertainment:** Appeals that use humour and entertainment aim to entertain and amuse the audience, eliciting laughter and enjoyment. These advertisements often rely on clever wordplay, visual gags, or situational comedy to create a memorable and engaging experience for viewers.
8. **Pride and Patriotism**: Appeals that evoke feelings of pride and patriotism appeal to consumers' sense of identity and belonging. These advertisements may celebrate cultural heritage, national pride, or community values, fostering a sense of unity and pride among the audience.
9. **Gratitude and Appreciation**: Appeals that express gratitude and appreciation aim to strengthen the bond between the brand and its customers. Whether thanking customers for their support, loyalty, or contributions,

these advertisements acknowledge the importance of the customer relationship and foster feelings of appreciation and goodwill.
10. **Hope and Optimism:** Appeals that inspire hope and optimism offer a sense of reassurance and encouragement, particularly in challenging or uncertain times. These advertisements may convey messages of resilience, perseverance, or the potential for positive change, inspiring consumers to look forward with optimism and confidence.

By understanding the different emotional appeals and their effects on consumers, brands can tailor their messaging and creative content to resonate with their target audience and achieve specific branding objectives.

Remember:

- **The Right Mix:** The most effective emotional appeals often use a combination of different emotions. Consider the overall message you want to convey and choose the emotions that best support it.
- **Subtlety can be Powerful:** Emotional appeals don't have to be over-the-top to be effective. Sometimes, a subtle touch can be even more impactful.
- **Testing and Refinement:** A/B testing different emotional appeals can help you determine what resonates most with your target audience. Don't be afraid to experiment and refine your approach.

Subaru: Love. It's What Makes a Subaru a Subaru

The "Love. It's what makes a Subaru a Subaru" campaign by Subaru is a powerful example of using emotional appeals in advertising to build an emotional brand connection.

At the heart of this campaign is the idea that Subaru isn't just selling cars—it's selling love—love for family, love for adventure, love for the great outdoors, and love for the brand itself. By positioning love as the core value and driving force behind Subaru, the brand taps into one of the most fundamental and universally resonant human emotions.

The advertisements in this campaign are masterfully crafted to evoke strong emotional responses from viewers. Many of the commercials feature heartwarming stories and vignettes that showcase the love shared within families, between partners, or between humans and their beloved pets. These slice-of-life narratives resonate deeply because they reflect the genuine bonds, joys, and challenges that people experience in their own lives.

One particularly poignant example is the "Baby Driver" commercial, which follows the journey of a father teaching his daughter to drive, culminating in her leaving for college. The ad beautifully captures the bittersweet emotion of a parent's love for their child and the inevitable moment when they must let them go. By weaving the Subaru vehicle into this deeply personal and relatable story, the brand creates an emotional association between its product and the profound love shared within a family.

Another powerful aspect of the "Love" campaign is its emphasis on adventure and exploration. Subaru positions itself as a brand that not only enables but also encourages its owners to pursue their love of the great outdoors, whether it's camping, hiking, or simply enjoying scenic drives. The advertisements feature breathtaking natural landscapes and depict families and friends creating cherished memories together while exploring the world around them. This appeal to wanderlust and the desire for authentic experiences taps into the human need for adventure, freedom, and connection with nature.

Moreover, Subaru's advertisements often showcase the love and loyalty that owners feel toward the brand itself. By highlighting the brand's reputation for safety, reliability, and capability, Subaru reinforces the idea that its vehicles are trusted companions on life's journey—an emotional bond that transcends mere transportation.

The "Love" campaign's success lies in its ability to seamlessly weave the Subaru brand into the fabric of deeply human experiences and emotions. Rather than simply touting features and specifications, the advertisements focus on the emotional resonance that Subaru aims to create for its customers.

Whether it's the love within a family, the love of adventure, or the love for the brand itself, Subaru's messaging taps into the universal human need for connection, belonging, and shared experiences.

By positioning love as the driving force behind its brand, Subaru has created a powerful emotional connection with its audience. The campaign acknowledges that consumers are not just rational decision-makers but complex human beings seeking fulfillment, meaning, and emotional resonance in their lives – and Subaru presents itself as the brand that can provide that sense of love and connection.

P&G's "Thank You, Mom" campaign

P&G's "Thank You, Mom" campaign, launched in conjunction with the Olympic Games, stands out as a prime example of leveraging emotional appeal in advertising to build a strong emotional brand. Since its debut in 2010, the campaign has struck a chord with audiences worldwide by paying tribute to the pivotal role of mothers in nurturing their children's aspirations and achievements.

At the heart of P&G's campaign is a celebration of gratitude and appreciation for mothers. Through heartfelt storytelling and poignant visuals, the campaign beautifully captures the unwavering support and sacrifices of mothers, evoking feelings of gratitude and admiration among viewers who hold their own mothers in high regard.

Moreover, the campaign taps into emotions of pride and inspiration by showcasing the dedication and sacrifices of mothers in supporting their children's dreams. By highlighting the unseen heroes behind every achievement, P&G instills a sense of pride and motivation in viewers, encouraging them to cherish and celebrate the influential figures in their lives.

Additionally, the campaign strategically incorporates elements of nostalgia and familiarity by featuring flashbacks to cherished childhood moments with mothers. This evokes feelings of warmth and connection, making the campaign relatable and universally appealing across cultures and backgrounds.

P&G's "Thank You, Mom" campaign goes beyond merely selling products; it fosters a deep emotional connection with audiences by celebrating the power of maternal love and support. This focus on human connection and shared experiences builds trust and loyalty towards the P&G brand, as viewers associate it with values of family, gratitude, and inspiration.

The campaign's success is evident in its significant impact on P&G's sales and brand image. By resonating with audiences worldwide and solidifying P&G's reputation as a company that values mothers and families, the campaign demonstrates the profound influence of emotional appeal in driving business results and building a lasting emotional brand.

Listerine

In the 1920s, Listerine revolutionized marketing by employing fear appeal to influence consumer behaviour. At the time, Listerine was marketed as a mouthwash solution to combat "halitosis," a term the brand popularized for bad breath. Listerine's strategic use of fear appeal was instrumental in its success. Here's how Listerine effectively employed this strategy:

Listerine's advertising campaigns preyed on people's fear of social rejection due to bad breath. They painted a vivid picture of the potential consequences of halitosis, such as losing friends, damaging romantic relationships, and facing rejection in both personal and professional spheres.

One of Listerine's most iconic ads featured a distressed young woman under the headline "Often a Bridesmaid, but Never a Bride." This advertisement suggested that bad breath could not only hinder social interactions but also jeopardize one's chances of getting married, playing on the fear of missing out on significant life milestones.

Listerine ads often depicted couples, implying that bad breath could lead to relationship breakdowns. For instance, one ad read, "Can you afford to be less popular than a skunk at a lawn party?" This negative imagery reinforced the fear that bad breath could damage personal connections.

Furthermore, Listerine ads suggested that bad breath could cost individuals job opportunities, tapping into the fear of professional failure due to halitosis.

To medicalize bad breath and amplify its seriousness, Listerine coined the term "halitosis." This linguistic tactic aimed to enhance the perceived severity of the problem.

Listerine's marketing strategy promised consumers that using its product could prevent these dire consequences. After instilling fear, the ads offered the promise of social acceptance, success in relationships, and career advancement through Listerine use.

Listerine's fear-based advertising approach was groundbreaking and highly effective. By emphasizing the potential negative outcomes of not using the product, Listerine exploited consumers' negativity bias.

"Mayhem" Commercials

State Farm's "Mayhem" commercials are a prime example of fear emotional appeal in advertising, expertly weaving together humour and relatability to drive home the importance of insurance protection. The campaign, featuring actor Dean Winters as the mischievous "Mayhem" character, cleverly taps into people's fears and anxieties surrounding worst-case scenarios while offering State Farm as the solution.

"Mayhem" embodies the worst-case scenarios that individuals fear while driving or protecting their property, bringing to life potential negative outcomes such as car accidents, home burglaries, and unexpected disasters. Through his chaotic and unpredictable behaviour, "Mayhem" triggers viewers' fear and anxiety, demonstrating the consequences of not being adequately prepared for unexpected events.

Dean Winters' portrayal of "Mayhem" humanizes the threats, making them relatable and more impactful. By becoming the embodiment of the negative events that can disrupt people's lives, "Mayhem" reinforces the idea that insurance is essential for safeguarding against life's uncertainties.

The humour and creativity of the "Mayhem" commercials make them highly memorable and shareable. By depicting accidents in a comedic way, the commercials evoke a lighthearted fear of what could happen without insurance, effectively engaging viewers without being overly distressing.

Despite the fear-inducing scenarios, the commercials always end with the solution – State Farm insurance. This creates a sense of relief and security for viewers, reinforcing the brand's role in protecting them from potential mishaps.

State Farm's "Mayhem" commercials strike a balance between fear and humor, effectively delivering their message while engaging a wide audience. Through relatable scenarios, humorous portrayals, and the promise of security, these commercials effectively leverage fear emotional appeal to drive home the importance of insurance protection.

The "Like a Girl" campaign by Always

Procter & Gamble's feminine hygiene brand Always tackled a sensitive and emotionally charged issue with its groundbreaking "Like a Girl" campaign – the negative connotations and insults often associated with the phrase "like a girl."

The centrepiece of this campaign was a thought-provoking video that began by asking adults to illustrate what it means to run, throw, or fight "like a girl." Their responses are filled with unflattering stereotypes and depictions of weakness and inadequacy. However, when the same question is posed to young girls, their answers are strikingly different – they demonstrate running, throwing, and fighting with confidence, strength, and determination.

This stark contrast powerfully highlights how the phrase "like a girl" becomes laden with negative connotations and damaging implications as girls grow older and encounter societal pressures and gender stereotypes. The video serves as an emotional wake-up call, challenging viewers to confront their own biases and redefine what it means to do something "like a girl" in a positive, empowering way.

Always' messaging throughout the campaign reinforced this theme of empowerment and self-confidence, urging girls and women to embrace their strength, resilience, and potential without letting harmful stereotypes hold them back. The brand positioned itself as a champion for girls' self-esteem and a force for positive change in how society perceives and values young women.

By tackling such an emotionally resonant and deeply personal issue, Always created a powerful emotional connection with its audience. The campaign acknowledged the very real struggles and insecurities that many girls and women face, validating their experiences and demonstrating that the brand truly understood and valued them as complex human beings.

Furthermore, Always' call to redefine and reclaim the phrase "like a girl" as a positive affirmation struck a chord with consumers who were eager to challenge negative stereotypes and promote a more inclusive, empowering narrative around gender and self-worth.

The emotional impact of the "Like a Girl" campaign was amplified through a robust social media strategy, where Always encouraged girls and women to share their own stories and experiences related to the campaign's message. This created a sense of community and shared purpose, further strengthening the emotional bond between the brand and its audience.

By fearlessly addressing a sensitive and emotionally charged issue, and by positioning itself as a champion for girls' self-esteem and empowerment, Always' "Like a Girl" campaign resonated deeply with consumers on an emotional level. The brand demonstrated its understanding of the struggles and aspirations of its audience, fostering a sense of authenticity and shared values that transcended the product itself.

Hope-based Emotional Appeal

It was early 1900s. Charles Pearce, a man with a vision, had a new soap in his hands. Crafted with a blend of palm and olive oils, it held the promise of something special. But the so-called experts scoffed, dismissing its advertising potential. Fear, they said, was the key to selling soap—fear of wrinkles, body odour, and a fading complexion.

Pearce, however, wasn't convinced. He sought the counsel of Claude Hopkins, a pioneer in advertising who believed hope, not fear, was the more powerful motivator. Hopkins saw the fear tactics employed by other soap companies and knew a different approach was needed.

Through research, Hopkins discovered a key insight: for his target audience, primarily women, the desire for beauty was a burning hope. At a time when beauty appeals in advertising were still a novelty, Hopkins saw his chance. He delved deeper, learning about Cleopatra, a historical icon renowned for her alluring beauty. Legend spoke of her bathing rituals, which included a blend of oils.

A spark ignited in Hopkins' mind. Here was the perfect way to tap into the hope for beauty – by connecting their new soap to Cleopatra's legendary routine. The ads he crafted were a testament to this strategy. They spoke of an "Egyptian beauty secret," a 3,000-year-old tradition revived for the modern woman. They promised not just cleansing, but the potential for a radiant, youthful glow.

In one ad, there was a picture of an Egyptian maid followed by the following content: "*The Egyptian maid of 3000 years was famous for her Perfect complexion—probably due to the use of Olive oil in combination with palm oil. We know that no other natural products have been discovered to equal Palm and Olive oils in benefit to the skin. Our scientific combination has developed its effectiveness in our Palmolive. Palmolive surpasses any other method for keeping the skin smooth, soft and beautiful.*"

In another ad, Hopkins says, "*All the world loves natural beauty. You can gain it in a simple way.......Palmolive. It has brought the enticement of fresh, clear skin to thousands.*"

This was the birth of the Palmolive campaign, a testament to the power of hope in advertising. It wasn't fear that would drive sales but the aspiration for a natural, captivating beauty attainable with every luxurious lather.

In conclusion, leveraging emotional appeal in advertisements is essential for building an emotional brand. By bypassing logic to connect with consumers on a deeper level, creating memorable experiences, fostering loyalty, differentiating from competitors, and humanizing the brand, emotional advertising plays a vital role in shaping consumer perceptions and driving brand success.

* * *

Conclusion

As we conclude our journey through the intricacies of building an emotional brand, it's evident that emotional connections lie at the heart of successful branding strategies. From recognizing consumers as humans with complex emotions to delving into their aspirations and values, each chapter has highlighted the importance of understanding and resonating with the emotional landscape of our audience.

We've explored the significance of gathering emotional insights during consumer research, emphasizing quality, consistency, and going beyond the core function to deliver memorable experiences. Personalization and habit-forming elements have been identified as key drivers of emotional engagement, while storytelling and authentic messaging have emerged as powerful tools for connecting with consumers on a deeper level.

Moreover, we've discussed the value of building relationships with customers, fostering communities of shared interests, and selling identity to align our brands with the aspirations and lifestyles of our target audience. Customer empowerment has been underscored as a cornerstone of emotional branding, enabling consumers to take ownership of their experiences and become advocates for our brands.

Finally, we've explored the role of emotional appeal in advertisements, recognizing its ability to bypass logic, build loyalty, differentiate from competitors, and humanize our brands.

As we reflect on these insights, it's clear that building an emotional brand is a multifaceted endeavor that requires empathy, creativity, and a deep understanding of human psychology. By prioritizing emotional connections, we can create brands that resonate with consumers on a profound level, driving loyalty, advocacy, and long-term success.

In essence, building an emotional brand is not just about selling products or services; it's about crafting meaningful experiences, fostering genuine relationships, and becoming a trusted companion on the journey of our consumers' lives. As we embark on this ongoing journey of emotional branding, let us continue to listen, empathize, and innovate, always striving to touch the hearts and minds of our audience in profound and lasting ways.

* * *

About the Author

Shah Mohammed is an accomplished Business Strategy and design-thinking consultant with a passion for innovation and user-centred design. He is the founder of D-Cube Designs, a leading design consultancy based in Chennai, India. With a Master's degree in Design from IIT Kanpur, India, which he obtained in 2004, Shah brings a strong academic background and a wealth of practical experience to his work.

As an Industrial Designer, Shah has played a pivotal role in successfully developing and launching over 300 products across various industries over the past decade. His expertise spans the entire product lifecycle, from conducting in-depth user research to designing intuitive and aesthetically pleasing solutions. Shah's keen understanding of customer needs and his ability to translate them into innovative product designs have earned him a reputation for excellence in the industry.

In addition to his contributions to the field of design, Shah has also established himself as a sought-after Business Strategy consultant. Leveraging his customer-centric approach, he has provided valuable insights and guidance to businesses of all sizes, helping them identify market opportunities, develop effective strategies, and drive growth. His expertise in areas such as branding, emotional branding, creativity techniques, leadership, and building competitive advantages has made him a trusted advisor to CEOs, startup founders, and aspiring entrepreneurs.

Shah is an avid blogger and has been sharing his knowledge and insights through his blog for the past six years. With over four hundred articles covering a wide range of topics, including Branding lessons, Design Thinking, Business Strategy, and Psychology in Business, his blog has become a valuable resource for professionals seeking practical advice and inspiration. The content featured in this book are a curated selection of some of his most impactful blogs, offering readers timeless lessons and actionable strategies.

You can connect with me on:
- https://shahmm.medium.com
- https://twitter.com/shahbaba
- https://www.linkedin.com/in/shahmm
- https://www.d-cubedesigns.com

Also by Shah Mohammed

Books on Brand Strategy, Business Strategy, Leadership, and Organizational Culture.

The Positioning Playbook: The Winning Strategies for Market Dominance

Unlock the secrets to market supremacy with "The Positioning Playbook: The Winning Strategies for Market Dominance." This comprehensive guide dives into the art and science of strategic positioning, revealing the proven strategies that will set your business apart from the competition and propel you to the top of your industry.

Discover the power of positioning, going beyond superficial branding and slogans, to create a deep and lasting impact on your target audience. Learn how to carve out a distinct space in consumers' minds, forging emotional connections and delivering unique value that resonates with their needs and desires.

Throughout the book, readers are introduced to thirteen effective positioning strategies, each serving as a pathway to achieving market dominance and sustainable success.

Boil The Ocean: The Story of World's Amazing Brands
Embark on a captivating journey through the world of iconic brands with "Boil The Ocean: The Story of World's Amazing Brands." This thought-provoking book offers a collection of insightful case studies that delve into the successes, failures, and transformative moments of some of the most renowned brands in history.

With meticulous research and captivating storytelling, "Boil The Ocean" offers valuable insights, timeless lessons, and inspiring narratives that will engage both business enthusiasts and casual readers. Whether you are an entrepreneur, marketer, designer, brand strategist, startup owner, CEO, brand consultant, or simply intrigued by the stories behind the brands we know and love, this book will leave you inspired, informed, and eager to explore the dynamic world of branding and business.

CEO ASAP: Insider Tips from TOP CEOs for Climbing the Corporate Ladder
Welcome to the ultimate guide for aspiring leaders and young professionals aiming to ascend the corporate ladder swiftly and confidently. "CEO ASAP" is your blueprint for success, curated from the wisdom and experiences of top CEOs who have paved the way to the corner office.

Workplace Whispers: Debunking Myths and Paradoxes
Workplace Whispers: Debunking Myths and Paradoxes" is a captivating exploration of the hidden narratives that shape our professional lives. Across its pages, "Workplace Whispers" examines a diverse array of myths and paradoxes that permeate modern organizational culture. From the allure of Simon Sinek's "Starting with Why" to the pitfalls of the Growth Mindset Myth, each chapter offers a fresh perspective on familiar concepts, prompting readers to question deeply held beliefs and assumptions.

The Secret Strategies of Marketing: How Brands Use Cognitive Biases to Win Your Wallet
In a world bombarded by marketing messages, understanding the psychology that underpins consumer behaviour is the ultimate game-changer. Whether you're a marketer, entrepreneur, business owner, or an inquisitive consumer, this book unravels the mysteries behind why certain brands resonate deeply while others remain forgettable.

Your Guide to Cognitive Biases: This comprehensive guide explores a treasure trove of cognitive biases, from the well-known to the lesser-explored, offering profound insights into their applications and impact. From the allure of familiarity to the power of scarcity, you'll journey through a spectrum of biases that influence every purchase decision.

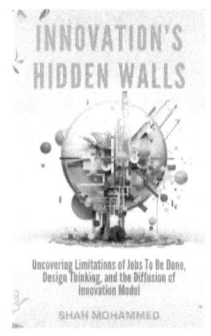
Innovation's Hidden Walls: Uncovering Limitations of Jobs To Be Done, Design Thinking, and the Diffusion of Innovation Model

In "Innovation's Hidden Walls," we delve deep into the core principles of Jobs To Be Done (JTBD), Design Thinking, and the Diffusion of Innovation Model. While these methodologies have been celebrated for sparking innovation, this book takes a critical look at their limitations. Discover how these walls can restrict your innovation endeavours, and learn how to break through them to truly transform your approach to problem-solving.

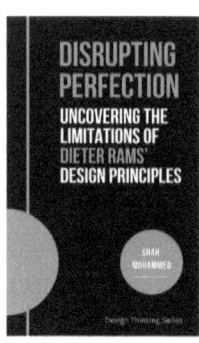
Disrupting Perfection: Uncovering the Limitations of Dieter Rams' Design Principles

"Disrupting Perfection" challenges the conventional wisdom surrounding Dieter Rams' celebrated design principles by delving into their limitations and exploring alternative perspectives on design excellence. This thought-provoking book critiques each of Rams' principles and presents compelling examples that challenge their applicability in contemporary design practice. Through insightful analysis and real-world case studies, readers are invited to reconsider established design norms and embrace a more nuanced understanding of design innovation and user experience.

SUB-BRANDING PLAYBOOK: Winning Strategies for Targeted Growth

In this captivating playbook, you'll discover a treasure trove of sub-branding strategies, each chapter unveiling a different secret weapon to unlock targeted growth. From creating sub-brands for demographic segmentation to psychographic targeting and cultural branding, we leave no stone unturned.

The book provides insights into successful sub-branding initiatives through real-world case studies, offering practical, actionable strategies for leveraging sub-brands to achieve targeted growth. By examining the considerations and criteria for developing sub-brands, readers can understand how sub-brands contribute to brand differentiation, customer targeting, and market expansion.

Elevate your brand's position, attract a loyal customer base, and surpass your competition. The Sub-Branding Playbook is your trusted companion on this exciting adventure, offering guidance, inspiration, and a roadmap to targeted growth.

Breaking Chains: A Manager's Playbook for Becoming a Leader
Embark on a transformative journey from managerial expertise to visionary leadership with "Breaking Chains: A Manager's Playbook for Becoming a Leader." This compelling book redefines leadership, offering invaluable insights and strategies for individuals striving to ascend from managerial roles to impactful leadership positions. Rooted in real-world scenarios and enriched by a wealth of leadership wisdom, this playbook provides a roadmap for professional growth and organizational success.

Unveiling the Managerial Metamorphosis: In the fast-paced landscape of contemporary business, the transition from a manager to a leader is a profound evolution. "Breaking Chains" explores this metamorphosis, unraveling the core shifts that propel individuals from functional mastery to strategic leadership. Drawing inspiration from Michael D. Watkins' HBR article, the playbook delves into transformative factors such as Specialist to Generalist, Analyst to Integrator, Tactician to Strategist, and so on.

www.ingramcontent.com/pod-product-compliance
Lightning Source LLC
Chambersburg PA
CBHW031627210526
45464CB00004B/1785